BAKING

Edited by
Jean Prince

octopus

Contents

This edition first published 1980 by
Octopus Books Limited
59 Grosvenor Street, London W.1.

© 1980 Octopus Books Limited

ISBN 0 7064 1343 1

Produced and printed in Hong Kong by
Mandarin Publishers Limited
22a Westlands Road, Quarry Bay

Cover photography by Paul Williams

Frontispiece: HAZEL NUTTIES *(page 55) (Photographer: Bryce Attwen)*

Weights and Measures

All measurements in this book are given in Metric, Imperial and American.

Measurements in weight in the Imperial and American system are the same. Liquid measurements are different, and the following table shows the equivalents:

Liquid measurements
1 Imperial pint .... 20 fluid ounces
1 American pint .... 16 fluid ounces
1 American cup .... 8 fluid ounces

Level spoon measurements
1 tablespoon... 15 ml
1 teaspoon .... 5 ml

Remember that the ingredients columns are not interchangeable. Follow only one set of measures.

INTRODUCTION

The delicious smell of freshly baked bread, cakes, scones, bun and biscuits is just one of the rewards to be gained from a home-baking session. You also have the satisfaction of knowing that every item costs less to bake than it would to buy and that it is one hundred percent wholesome! Add to that the appreciative murmurs of the family and it all becomes very worth while.

Once you've established a routine, you will be surprised to find how simple and speedy baking can be. Never again will you queue for hours if there's a threatened bread shortage, or over buy before bank holidays on the principle that it is better to have too much than too little. Instead, you can keep a bag of plain or wholewheat flour in the storecupboard, some fresh yeast in the refrigerator or active dried yeast in an airtight can, and you will have no more problems.

I have said that baking is simple, and so it is, but here are a few helpful pointers to bear in mind – first about bread.
Kneading: all yeast doughs must be kneaded after mixing until they become smooth and elastic; this is to ensure a good texture and well-risen bread. During the two rising periods it should be covered to prevent a skin forming on the surface, and should be twice its original volume before you place it in the oven. If you want the dough to rise quickly, place it in a warm place (but not too warm); for a slower rise, place it in the refrigerator. Knocking-back: shaping the risen dough by kneading it with the knuckles for one to two minutes to knock out air bubbles before the second rising; this ensures that it rises evenly.
Proving: the second rising of the dough, after it has been knocked back.

If you want a really crisp crust, transfer loaves from their tins to a baking sheet for the final 5 minutes of the baking time. A cooked loaf sounds hollow when tapped on the base with the knuckles.

Baking cakes is equally rewarding, and a little artistry can transform the most simple cake into a party centrepiece (centerpiece) by the addition of an appropriate decoration. In the section on celebration cakes there are two very good basic recipes that lend themselves to all kinds of decoration, and are just as delicious left unadorned! Once you have enjoyed a few successes by following these recipes to the letter, you will have the confidence to experiment on your own with various flavourings and fillings, toppings and colourings.

Always grease or line the baking tins (pans). A properly cooked cake should be well-risen, golden brown and slightly shrunk from the sides of the tin (pan). A sponge or creamed cake is done when it springs lightly back if the top is gently pressed with the fingertips. Large, deep cakes are cooked when a warm skewer, inserted into the centre (center) of the cake, comes out clean. Cakes should be stored in air-tight tins; the storage time varies according to the type of cake.

From top: APPLE AND ALMOND FLAN *(page 11)*, CHESTNUT
LAYER GATEAU *(page 23)*, MINCEMEAT PLAIT *(page 10)*
(Photograph: Birds Eye Kitchens)

FAMILY CAKES

Mincemeat Plait

METRIC/IMPERIAL	AMERICAN
225 g/8 oz mincemeat	*1 cup mincemeat*
50 g/2 oz glacé cherries, chopped	*¼ cup chopped candied cherries*
50 g/2 oz almonds, blanched and chopped	*½ cup blanched and chopped almonds*
1 × 400 g/14 oz packet frozen puff pastry, thawed	*1 × 1 lb package frozen puff paste, thawed*
To glaze:	**To glaze:**
1 egg, beaten	*1 egg, beaten*
Icing:	**Frosting:**
100 g/4 oz sifted icing sugar	*1 cup sifted confectioners' sugar*
1 tablespoon lemon juice	*1 tablespoon lemon juice*
To decorate:	**To decorate:**
extra chopped glacé cherries and blanched almonds	*extra chopped candied cherries and blanched almonds*

Combine the mincemeat, glacé cherries (candied cherries) and almonds for the filling. Roll out the pastry (paste) to an oblong 30 × 35 cm/12 × 14 in. Lightly mark it into three, lengthwise. Brush the edges of the pastry (paste) with water. Make 7 cm/3 in cuts, 2.5 cm/1 in apart at an angle of 45° along the edges. Place the filling down the centre third and fold strips over alternately to give a plaited effect. Seal the ends. Place on a baking sheet. Glaze with beaten egg and bake in a preheated hot oven (220°C/425°F, Gas Mark 7) for 20 minutes. Cool.

Blend together the icing sugar (confectioners' sugar) and lemon juice, adding a little boiling water to give a smooth glacé icing (frosting). Spoon over the plait and sprinkle with the cherries and almonds.
Serves 6

Cut and Come Again Cake

METRIC/IMPERIAL	AMERICAN
100 g/4 oz butter	$\frac{1}{2}$ cup butter
100 g/4 oz sugar	$\frac{1}{2}$ cup sugar
1 egg, beaten	1 egg, beaten
225 g/8 oz self-raising flour	2 cups self-rising flour
$\frac{1}{2}$ teaspoon salt	$\frac{1}{2}$ teaspoon salt
1 teaspoon mixed spice	1 teaspoon mixed spice
120 ml/4 fl oz milk	$\frac{1}{2}$ cup milk
250 g/9 oz mixed dried fruit	$1\frac{1}{2}$ cups mixed dried fruit
1 teaspoon grated orange rind	1 teaspoon grated orange rind

Cream together the butter and sugar in a bowl until light and fluffy. Add the egg, a little at a time and mix well. Mix in the flour, salt and spice. Stir in the milk, fruit and rind. Turn the mixture into a greased and bottom-lined 1 kg/2 lb loaf tin (loaf pan). Bake on the middle shelf of a preheated moderate oven (180°C/350°F, Gas Mark 4) for $1\frac{1}{2}$ hours or until a warm skewer comes out clean. Cool on a wire rack.
Makes one 1 kg/2 lb cake

Apple and Almond Flan (Pie)

METRIC/IMPERIAL	AMERICAN
1 × 225 g/8 oz packet frozen shortcrust pastry, thawed	1 × $\frac{1}{2}$ lb package frozen basic pie dough, thawed
2 cooking apples, peeled and sliced	2 baking apples, peeled and sliced
50 g/2 oz ground almonds	$\frac{1}{2}$ cup ground almonds
50 g/2 oz soft brown sugar	$\frac{1}{3}$ cup light brown sugar
1 teaspoon ground cinnamon	1 teaspoon ground cinnamon
300 ml/10 fl oz soured cream	$1\frac{1}{4}$ cups sour cream
1 tablespoon icing sugar	1 tablespoon confectioners' sugar

Roll out the pastry (dough) and line a 20 cm/8 in flan ring (pie ring). Bake 'blind' in a preheated moderately hot oven (190°C/375°F, Gas Mark 5) for 20 minutes, removing the beans after 10 minutes.

Meanwhile, cook the apples, almonds, brown sugar and cinnamon until soft. Spoon the mixture into the flan ring (pie ring). Pour the cream over the top. Use the remaining pastry to make eight thin strips to form a lattice over the flan. Return to the oven and bake until set, about 30 to 40 minutes. Cool. Sprinkle with icing sugar (confectioners' sugar). Serve with cream.
Makes one 20 cm/8 in round flan (pie)

Chocolate Potato Cake

METRIC/IMPERIAL
100 g/4 oz butter
175 g/6 oz caster sugar
75 g/3 oz potatoes, cooked, mashed
  and sieved
40 g/1½ oz chocolate
2 eggs
175 g/6 oz self-raising flour, sifted
4 tablespoons milk
Filling:
50 g/2 oz butter
75 g/3 oz icing sugar, sifted
25 g/1 oz cocoa, sifted
To decorate:
icing sugar
glacé cherries

AMERICAN
½ cup butter
¾ cup sugar
⅓ cup cooked, mashed and strained
  potatoes
1½ squares chocolate
2 eggs
1½ cups self-rising flour, sifted
4 tablespoons milk
Filling:
¼ cup butter
¾ cup confectioners' sugar
¼ cup unsweetened cocoa, sifted
To decorate:
confectioners' sugar
candied cherries

Cream the butter and sugar thoroughly, add the mashed potatoes and mix well together. Melt the chocolate and add to the creamed mixture. Beat the eggs and stir in. Add the flour and blend well together. Gradually add the milk and mix well to form a soft dropping consistency.

Divide the mixture evenly between two 18 cm/7 in cake tins (cake pans) and bake in a preheated moderately hot oven (190°C/375°F, Gas Mark 5) for 25 to 30 minutes. The cake is cooked when it is quite firm but springy on top when pressed lightly. Turn out on to a wire tray to cool.

Place the filling ingredients in a bowl and mix well until the icing sugar (confectioners' sugar) and cocoa are completely blended. Sandwich the cake together with this chocolate butter icing.

Sift a fine film of icing sugar (confectioners' sugar) over the top of the cake, evenly space 9 glacé cherries (candied cherries) round the edge of the cake and place remaining cherry in the centre.
Makes one 18 cm/7 in round cake

CHOCOLATE POTATO CAKE *(Photograph: Potato Marketing Board)*

Boiled Fruit Cake

METRIC/IMPERIAL	AMERICAN
100 g/4 oz margarine	$\frac{1}{2}$ cup margarine
425 g/1 lb mixed dried fruit	3 cups mixed dried fruit
225 g/8 oz soft brown sugar	$1\frac{1}{3}$ cups light brown sugar
150 ml/$\frac{1}{4}$ pint water	$\frac{2}{3}$ cup water
2 eggs, beaten	2 eggs, beaten
225 g/8 oz self-raising flour	2 cups self-rising flour

Put the margarine, fruit, sugar and water into a large saucepan. Bring to the boil and simmer for 15 to 20 minutes with the lid on. Allow to cool. Mix in the beaten eggs and flour. Turn into a greased and lined 18 cm/7 in round cake tin (pan). Bake in a preheated cool oven (150°C/300°F, Gas Mark 2) for $1\frac{1}{2}$ to 2 hours, or until a warm skewer comes out clean when inserted into the centre of the cake. Turn out and cool on a wire rack.

Makes one 18 cm/7 in round cake

Marmalade Cheesecake

METRIC/IMPERIAL	AMERICAN
50 g/2 oz butter	$\frac{1}{4}$ cup butter
100 g/4 oz digestive biscuits, crushed	1 cup crushed Graham crackers
3 eggs, separated	3 eggs, separated
175 g/6 oz caster sugar	$\frac{3}{4}$ cup sugar
225 g/8 oz cream cheese	1 cup cream cheese
2 tablespoons lemon juice	2 tablespoons lemon juice
3 tablespoons fine cut marmalade	3 tablespoons fine cut marmalade
15 g/$\frac{1}{2}$ oz gelatine	2 envelopes gelatin
3 tablespoons hot water	3 tablespoons hot water
150 ml/$\frac{1}{4}$ pint double cream	$\frac{2}{3}$ cup heavy cream
To decorate:	**To decorate:**
strips of marmalade rind	strips of marmalade rind

Grease and line a loose-bottomed 18 cm/7 in cake tin (springform pan). Melt the butter, stir in the biscuits (Graham crackers) and press lightly into the base of the cake tin (springform pan).

Beat together the egg yolks and sugar, add the cream cheese and beat until smooth. Stir in the lemon juice and marmalade. Dissolve the gelatine (gelatin) in the hot water and stir into the mixture. Whisk the egg whites until fairly stiff, lightly whip the cream; fold both into the mixture. Pour into the cake tin (springform pan) and leave to set in a cool place. Decorate with strips of marmalade rind.

Makes one 18 cm/7 in round cheesecake

Golden Savarin

METRIC/IMPERIAL

Yeast batter:
25 g/1 oz strong plain white flour
2 teaspoons dried yeast
1 teaspoon sugar
150 ml/¼ pint warm milk

Dough:
75 g/3 oz strong plain white flour
pinch of salt
15 g/½ oz caster sugar
50 g/2 oz ground almonds
50 g/2 oz raisins
50 g/2 oz butter
1 egg beaten

Syrup:
225 g/8 oz caster sugar
300 ml/½ pint water

Filling:
3 to 4 oranges, peeled and segmented
150 ml/¼ pint double cream, whipped

AMERICAN

Yeast batter:
¼ cup all-purpose flour
2 teaspoons active dry yeast
1 teaspoon sugar
⅔ cup warm milk

Dough:
¾ cup all-purpose flour
pinch of salt
1 tablespoon firmly packed sugar
½ cup ground almonds
6 tablespoons raisins
¼ cup butter
1 egg, beaten

Syrup:
1 cup firmly packed sugar
1¼ cups water

Filling:
3 to 4 oranges, peeled and segmented
⅔ cup heavy cream, whipped

Blend the batter ingredients together in a large bowl. Cover and leave in a warm place for 20 minutes until frothy.

To prepare the dough, combine the flour with the salt and sugar, almonds and raisins. Rub in the butter. Add the egg and flour mixture to the batter and mix well to form a very soft dough. Pour the mixture into a well greased 18 to 20 cm/7 to 8 in ring tin (pan). Cover with lightly oiled polythene (plastic) and leave to rise in a warm place until the dough reaches the top of the tin (pan).

Uncover and bake in a preheated moderately hot oven (200°C/400°F, Gas Mark 6) for 20 to 25 minutes until golden brown and springy to the touch. Turn out the savarin on to a wire rack placed over a dish.

To make the syrup, dissolve the sugar in the water over gentle heat. Increase the heat and boil until the temperature reaches 230°F. Remove from the heat, then slowly spoon the syrup over the savarin until it is absorbed. Allow the savarin to cool, then place on a serving dish. Fill the centre of the savarin with the orange segments and decorate the edge with piped cream.

Serves 4

Walnut Layer Cake

METRIC/IMPERIAL	AMERICAN
175 g/6 oz margarine	$\frac{3}{4}$ cup margarine
75 g/3 oz light soft brown sugar	$\frac{1}{2}$ cup light brown sugar
75 g/3 oz golden syrup	$\frac{1}{3}$ cup maple syrup
3 eggs, beaten	3 eggs, beaten
175 g/6 oz self-raising flour	$1\frac{1}{2}$ cups self-rising flour
100 g/4 oz walnuts, chopped	1 cup chopped walnuts
Filling:	**Filling:**
100 g/4 oz butter	$\frac{1}{2}$ cup butter
225 g/8 oz icing sugar, sifted	2 cups sifted confectioners' sugar
50 g/2 oz walnuts, chopped	$\frac{1}{2}$ cup chopped walnuts
American frosting:	**American frosting:**
225 g/8 oz caster sugar	1 cup firmly packed sugar
4 tablespoons water	4 tablespoons water
1 egg white	1 egg white
To decorate:	**To decorate:**
few walnut halves	few walnuts halves

Cream the margarine, sugar and syrup together until soft and light. Add the eggs gradually. Fold in the flour and the chopped nuts. Divide the mixture between three 18 cm/7 in greased and lined sandwich tins (layer cake pans). Bake in a preheated moderately hot oven (190°C/375°F, Gas Mark 5) for 20 to 25 minutes.

For the filling, cream together the butter and icing sugar (confectioners' sugar) until soft. Stir in the chopped nuts. Sandwich the layers together with this butter cream.

For the American frosting, heat the sugar and water together until dissolved. Bring to the boil without stirring and boil until 120°C/240°F. Whisk the egg white until stiff. Pour the syrup slowly on to the egg white and whisk all the time until the mixture thickens. Spread over the cake quickly and decorate with walnut halves.

Makes one 18 cm/7 in round cake

WALNUT LAYER CAKE *(Photographer: Paul Williams)*

Granny's Loaf

METRIC/IMPERIAL
225 g/8 oz self-raising flour
½ teaspoon salt
25 g/1 oz soft brown sugar
50 g/2 oz chopped walnuts
75 g/3 oz raisins
1 tablespoon golden syrup
150 ml/¼ pint milk

AMERICAN
2 cups self-rising flour
½ teaspoon salt
2 tablespoons light brown sugar
½ cup chopped walnuts
½ cup raisins
1 tablespoon maple syrup
⅔ cup milk

Place the dry ingredients together in a bowl, add the nuts and raisins. Stir in the golden syrup (maple syrup) and milk and beat to a very soft consistency. Turn into a greased and bottom lined 15 cm/6 in round cake tin (cake pan). Bake in a preheated moderate oven (180°C/350°F, Gas Mark 4) for about 45 minutes until the cake is well risen and has begun to shrink from the sides of the tin (pan). Turn on to a wire rack.
Makes one 15 cm/6 in round cake

Date and Walnut Cake

METRIC/IMPERIAL
225 g/8 oz plain flour
1 teaspoon baking powder
100 g/4 oz soft margarine
100 g/4 oz caster sugar
100 g/4 oz dates, chopped
50 g/2 oz walnuts, chopped
1 egg, beaten
1 teaspoon bicarbonate of soda
2 to 3 tablespoons milk

AMERICAN
2 cups all-purpose flour
1 teaspoon baking powder
½ cup soft margarine
½ cup sugar
⅔ cup chopped dates
½ cup chopped walnuts
1 egg, beaten
1 teaspoon baking soda
2 to 3 tablespoons milk

Grease and flour a 500 g/1 lb loaf tin (loaf pan). Place the flour, baking powder, margarine, sugar, dates, walnuts and egg in a large mixing bowl. Mix together the bicarbonate of soda (baking soda) and milk, add to the mixture and mix together until well blended. Spoon the mixture into the prepared tin, smoothing over the surface. Bake in a preheated moderate oven (180°C/350°F, Gas Mark 4) for 1¼ hours, until firm to the touch.

Allow the cake to cool in the tin (pan), then remove and place on a wire rack. This cake can be served as it is, or, for a special occasion, decorate with dates and walnuts and glaze with a little warm honey.
Makes one 500 g/1 lb cake

Cherry Cake

METRIC/IMPERIAL	AMERICAN
175 g/6 oz margarine	$\frac{3}{4}$ cup margarine
175 g/6 oz caster sugar	$\frac{3}{4}$ cup sugar
3 eggs	3 eggs
225 g/8 oz plain flour, sifted	2 cups all-purpose flour, sifted
50 g/2 oz cornflour, sifted	$\frac{1}{2}$ cup cornstarch, sifted
2 teaspoons baking powder	2 teaspoons baking powder
100 g/4 oz glacé cherries	$\frac{1}{2}$ cup candied cherries

Grease an 18 cm/7 in cake tin (cake pan). Cream together the margarine and sugar until light and creamy. Gradually beat in the eggs. Fold in the flour, cornflour (cornstarch) and baking powder and stir in half the cherries, chopped.

Place the mixture in the prepared cake tin (pan), cut the remainder of the cherries in half and arrange on top. Bake in a preheated moderate oven (160°C/325°F, Gas Mark 3) for $1\frac{1}{4}$ to $1\frac{1}{2}$ hours until well risen and golden brown. Remove and cool on a wire rack.

Makes one 18 cm/7 in round cake

Sandcake

METRIC/IMPERIAL	AMERICAN
175 g/6 oz butter	$\frac{3}{4}$ cup butter
175 g/6 oz caster sugar	$\frac{3}{4}$ cup sugar
3 eggs	3 eggs
100 g/4 oz plain flour, sifted	1 cup all-purpose flour, sifted
100 g/4 oz cornflour	1 cup cornstarch
1 teaspoon baking powder	1 teaspoon baking powder
$\frac{1}{2}$ teaspoon vanilla essence	$\frac{1}{2}$ teaspoon vanilla extract
2 tablespoons milk	2 tablespoons milk
25 g/1 oz flaked almonds	$\frac{1}{4}$ cup slivered almonds

Line a 1 kg/2 lb loaf tin (pan) with greased greaseproof paper (or non-stick parchment).

Cream the butter and sugar together until light and fluffy; beat in the eggs. Carefully fold in the flour, cornflour (cornstarch) and baking powder. Add the vanilla essence (extract) and about 2 tablespoons milk to give a dropping consistency.

Place the mixture in the loaf tin (pan), level the surface and sprinkle with the almonds. Bake in a preheated moderate oven (180°C/350°F, Gas Mark 4) for $1\frac{1}{4}$ hours or until firm to the touch. Remove cake, peel off the paper (parchment) and allow cake to cool on a wire rack.

Makes one 1 kg/2 lb cake

Treacle Tart

METRIC/IMPERIAL	AMERICAN
175 g/6 oz plain flour	*1½ cups all-purpose flour*
pinch of salt	*pinch of salt*
40 g/1½ oz butter	*3 tablespoons butter*
40 g/1½ oz lard	*3 tablespoons shortening*
2 to 3 tablespoons water	*2 to 3 tablespoons water*
Filling:	**Filling:**
4 tablespoons golden syrup	*4 tablespoons maple syrup*
4 tablespoons black treacle	*4 tablespoons molasses*
juice of ½ lemon	*juice of ½ lemon*
50 g/2 oz white breadcrumbs	*1 cup white bread crumbs*
milk to glaze	*milk to glaze*

Sift the flour and salt into a bowl and rub in the fats until the mixture resembles fine breadcrumbs. Add the water, mix to a firm dough. Roll out on a floured surface and use to cover a 20 to 23 cm/8 to 9 in pie plate.

Warm the syrup and treacle (molasses) with the lemon juice in a pan, stirring. Add the breadcrumbs and mix well. Pour into the pastry case (pie shell). Roll out pastry trimmings, cut into long strips and make a lattice. Brush pastry with milk and bake in a preheated moderately hot oven (200°C/400°F, Gas Mark 6) for 20 to 30 minutes.

Makes one 20 to 23 cm/8 to 9 in tart

TREACLE TART *(Photograph: The Flour Advisory Bureau)*

SPONGES AND GATEAUX

Redcurrant Layer Cake

METRIC/IMPERIAL	AMERICAN
100 g/4 oz butter	$\frac{1}{2}$ cup butter
100 g/4 oz caster sugar	$\frac{1}{2}$ cup sugar
2 eggs	2 eggs
100 g/4 oz self-raising flour, sifted	1 cup sifted self-rising flour
450 g/1 lb fresh red currants	1 lb fresh red currants
150 ml/$\frac{1}{4}$ pint double cream	$\frac{2}{3}$ cup heavy cream
Custard filling:	**Custard filling:**
250 ml/$\frac{1}{2}$ pint milk	$1\frac{1}{4}$ cups milk
1 vanilla pod	1 vanilla bean
1 egg	1 egg
1 egg yolk	1 egg yolk
50 g/2 oz caster sugar	$\frac{1}{4}$ cup sugar
25 g/1 oz plain flour	$\frac{1}{4}$ cup all-purpose flour

Cream the butter and sugar together. Beat in the eggs and fold in the flour. Divide the mixture between two greased 18 cm/7 in sandwich tins (layer cake pans). Bake in a preheated moderately hot oven (190°C/375°F, Gas Mark 5) for 20 to 25 minutes. Remove from the sandwich tins (layer cake pans) and cool on a wire rack.

To make the filling, bring the milk to the boil with the vanilla pod (bean) and gradually stir the milk into the mixture. Bring to the boil, stirring. Cook for 2 minutes and leave to cool.

String the red currants and reserve 100 g/4 oz/1 cup of the whole berries for decoration. Crush the remainder. Whip the cream until softly stiff. Cut the cakes in half, horizontally. Sandwich the cakes together with one third of the crushed redcurrants and custard filling spread between each layer. Spread the cream over the top and liberally sprinkle with the whole berries.

Makes one 18 cm/7 in cake

Chestnut Layer Gâteau

METRIC/IMPERIAL
1 × 400 g/14 oz packet frozen puff
pastry, thawed
1 × 225 g/8 oz can chestnut purée
300 ml/½ pint double cream
100 g/4 oz plain chocolate
50 g/2 oz sifted icing sugar

AMERICAN
1 × 1 lb package frozen puff paste,
thawed
1 × ½ lb can chestnut purée
1¼ cups heavy cream
4 squares semi-sweet chocolate pieces
½ cup sifted confectioners' sugar

Roll out the pastry (paste) thinly and cut into three 18 cm/7 in circles. Transfer onto greased baking sheets and prick. Bake in a preheated hot oven (220°C/425°F, Gas Mark 7) for 12 to 15 minutes until golden brown. Allow to cool.

Meanwhile, melt the chocolate and place the chestnut purée, double cream (heavy cream), half the melted chocolate and the icing sugar (confectioners' sugar) in a bowl and whisk together until thick. Trim the pastry (paste) circles to an even size and cover one with some of the cream mixture. Place the second circle on top and cover with more cream mixture. Place the last circle of pastry (paste) on top and cover with the remaining chocolate. Decorate with the remaining cream. Serve as soon as possible.

Makes one 18 cm /7 in round gâteau

Grape and Lemon Gâteau

METRIC/IMPERIAL

175 g/6 oz soft margarine
225 g/8 oz caster sugar
4 large eggs, beaten
225 g/8 oz self-raising flour

Filling:
300 ml/½ pint double cream
150 ml/¼ pint single cream
6 tablespoons lemon curd
2 tablespoons lemon juice
*225 g/8 oz green grapes, depipped
 and chopped*

To decorate:
50 g/2 oz walnuts, chopped
15 whole green grapes
caster sugar
egg white

AMERICAN

¾ cup soft margarine
1 cup firmly packed sugar
4 large eggs, beaten
2 cups self-rising flour

Filling:
1¼ cups heavy cream
⅔ cup light cream
6 tablespoons lemon curd
2 tablespoons lemon juice
*2 cups pitted and chopped white
 grapes*

To decorate:
½ cup chopped walnuts
15 whole white grapes
sugar
egg white

Place all the sponge cake ingredients in a bowl and, using a wooden spoon, beat well for three minutes. Divide the mixture between two greased and floured 20 cm/8 in sandwich tins (layer cake pans). Bake in a preheated moderately hot oven (190°C/375°F, Gas Mark 5) for 20 to 30 minutes until well risen and firm to the touch. Remove from the cake tins (cake pans) and cool on a wire rack.

To prepare the filling, place all the ingredients, except the grapes, in a bowl and whisk together until thick. Combine 6 tablespoons of this mixture with the chopped grapes.

Cut each cake in two horizontally, making four layers. Use two-thirds of the cream and grape mixture to sandwich them together. Spread a little of the remaining lemon cream lightly on the sides of the cake and coat with the chopped nuts. Spread the remainder of the lemon cream over the top of the cake, mark swirls with a knife or fork and decorate with a few whole grapes dipped in egg white and sugar, placing 3 at the centre and evenly spacing the remaining 12 grapes in pairs round the edge of the cake.

Makes one 20 cm/8 in round cake

GRAPE AND LEMON GATEAU (*Photograph: The Homepride Kitchen*)

Chocolate Feather Cake

METRIC/IMPERIAL

Cake:

175 g/6 oz margarine

175 g/6 oz caster sugar

175 g/6 oz self-raising flour sifted
  with 1½ teaspoons baking powder

2 tablespoons cocoa powder blended
  with 3 tablespoons warm water

3 large eggs

Filling:

40 g/1½ oz margarine

100 g/4 oz icing sugar, sifted

1 tablespoon orange juice

orange colouring (optional)

To decorate:

175 g/6 oz icing sugar, sifted

1½ to 2 tablespoons warm water

few drops orange colouring

AMERICAN

Cake:

¾ cup margarine

¾ cup sugar

1½ cups all-purpose flour sifted with
  1½ teaspoons baking powder

2 tablespoons unsweetened cocoa
  blended with 3 tablespoons warm
  water

3 large eggs

Filling:

3 tablespoons margarine

1 cup sifted confectioners' sugar

1 tablespoon orange juice

orange coloring (optional)

To decorate:

1⅓ cups sifted confectioners' sugar

1½ to 2 tablespoons warm water

few drops orange coloring

Place all the cake ingredients into a mixing bowl. Beat with a wooden spoon until well mixed, 2 to 3 minutes. Divide the mixture (batter) between two greased and bottom-lined 20 cm/8 in round cake tins (cake pans). Bake in the centre of a preheated moderate oven (160°C/325°F, Gas Mark 3) for 40 to 45 minutes. Turn out and cool on a wire rack before icing (frosting).

To make the filling, place all the filling ingredients in a mixing bowl and beat with a wooden spoon until well mixed. Use to sandwich the two cake halves together.

To make the glacé icing (frosting), place the icing sugar (confectioners' sugar) and warm water in a mixing bowl and beat with a wooden spoon until smooth. Reserve a little of the icing (frosting) and colour orange. Spread the white glacé icing (frosting) over the top of the cake. While still wet, pipe orange circles on the cake and drag a skewer backwards and forwards across the cake to form feather icing (frosting).

Makes one 20 cm/8 in round cake

Lemon and Chocolate Cake

METRIC/IMPERIAL

Cake:
175 g/6 oz margarine
175 g/6 oz caster sugar
3 eggs
175 g/6 oz self-raising flour
1½ teaspoons baking powder
1 tablespoon cocoa and 2 tablespoons
  water, blended

Icing:
75 g/3 oz margarine
225 g/8 oz icing sugar, sifted
grated rind and juice of 1 lemon

To decorate:
50 g/2 oz chocolate, grated or flaked
crystallized lemon slices

AMERICAN

Cake:
¾ cup margarine
¾ cup sugar
3 eggs
1½ cups self-rising flour
1½ teaspoons baking powder
1 tablespoon unsweetened cocoa and
  2 tablespoons water, blended

Frosting:
⅓ cup margarine
2 cups sifted confectioners' sugar
grated rind and juice of 1 lemon

To decorate:
2 squares semi-sweet grated or flaked
  chocolate
candied lemon slices

Place all the cake ingredients in a mixing bowl and beat together with a wooden spoon for 2 to 3 minutes until well mixed. Divide the mixture between two greased and bottom-lined 18 cm/8 in sandwich tins (layer cake pans). Bake in a preheated moderate oven (160°C/325°F, Gas Mark 3) for 30 to 40 minutes. Cool on a wire rack.

Place the icing (frosting) ingredients into a mixing bowl and beat together with a wooden spoon until smooth. Use half the icing (frosting) mixture to sandwich the cake together and spread the remaining icing (frosting) over the top of the cake, using a palette knife to give a swirling effect. Sprinkle grated or flaked chocolate around the top edge of the cake and decorate with lemon slices.

Makes one 18 cm/7 in round cake

Apricot Sunflower Gâteau

METRIC/IMPERIAL	AMERICAN
1 frozen round cream sponge cake	*1 frozen round cream sponge cake*
1 × 425 g/15 oz can apricot halves	*1 × 1 lb can apricot halves*
1 tablespoon custard powder	*1 tablespoon custard powder*
a little icing sugar	*a little confectioners' sugar*

While it is still frozen, cut the cake in half horizontally, through the cream. Cut a 9 cm/3½ in diameter circle from the centre of the top half; reserve, carefully replacing the remaining outer 'ring', cream side uppermost, on top of the uncut half. Leave to thaw.

Drain and reserve the syrup from the apricots and arrange most of the halves, rounded side up, around the top 'ring', chop remainder.

Blend the custard powder with the syrup and bring to the boil, stirring. Simmer for 3 minutes. Glaze the ring of apricots with some of this sauce. Add the chopped fruit to the remainder and cool, then spoon the mixture into the centre of the cake and top with the reserved sponge circle. Dust with icing sugar (confectioners' sugar) and serve at once.
Serves 6

Victoria Sandwich Cake

(Basic all-in-one recipe)

METRIC/IMPERIAL	AMERICAN
175 g/6 oz self-raising flour	*1½ cups self-rising flour*
1½ teaspoons baking powder	*1½ teaspoons baking powder*
175 g/6 oz margarine	*¾ cup margarine*
175 g/6 oz caster sugar	*¾ cup sugar*
3 large eggs	*3 large eggs*
Basic recipe for icing:	**Basic recipe for frosting:**
75 g/3 oz margarine	*⅓ cup margarine*
225 g/8 oz icing sugar, sifted	*2 cups sifted confectioners' sugar*
2 tablespoons milk or fruit juice	*2 tablespoons milk or fruit juice*

Sift together the flour and baking powder into a mixing bowl, then add the margarine, sugar and eggs. Beat with a wooden spoon until well-mixed. Divide the mixture between two greased and bottom-lined 18 cm/7 in round sandwich tins (layer cake pans). Bake in the centre of a preheated moderate oven (160°C/325°F, Gas Mark 3) for 45 minutes. Turn out and cool on a wire rack.

Place all the icing (frosting) ingredients in a bowl and beat together with a wooden spoon until well mixed. This quantity will fill the sandwich cake, and coat the sides and top.
Makes one 18 cm/7 in round cake

SUNSHINE GATEAU *(page 30) (Photograph: Stork Cookery Service)*

Sunshine Gâteau

METRIC/IMPERIAL	AMERICAN
1 quantity Victoria Sandwich cake mixture (see basic recipe, page 28)	1 quantity Victoria Sandwich cake batter (see basic recipe, page 28)
Filling:	**Filling:**
150 ml/¼ pint double cream	⅔ cup heavy cream
To decorate:	**To decorate:**
1 tablespoon sieved apricot jam	1 tablespoon strained apricot jam
1 banana	1 banana
little lemon juice	little lemon juice
100 g/4 oz black grapes	1 cup purple grapes
a few mandarin oranges	a few mandarin oranges

Bake two 18 cm/7 in round Victoria Sandwich cakes (see basic recipe, page 28). Lightly whip the cream. Cut each of the cakes in half horizontally, then sandwich them all together with a third of the cream between each layer. Spread the jam over top of cake. Slice the banana thinly and dip into lemon juice to prevent discoloring, then use the fruits to decorate top of cake, as shown on page 29.

Makes one 18 cm/7 in round cake

Chequer–Board Cake

METRIC/IMPERIAL	AMERICAN
1 quantity Victoria Sandwich mixture (see page 28)	1 quantity Victoria Sandwich batter (see page 28)
Filling and decoration:	**Filling and decoration:**
¼ teaspoon almond essence	¼ teaspoon almond extract
1 quantity basic icing (page 28)	1 quantity basic frosting (page 28)
50 g/2 oz glacé cherries, chopped	¼ cup chopped candied cherries
25 g/1 oz walnuts, chopped	¼ cup chopped walnuts
25 g/1 oz blanched almonds, chopped	¼ cup chopped blanched almonds
2 teaspoons cocoa powder	2 teaspoons unsweetened cocoa
1 teaspoon hot water	1 teaspoon hot water

Bake two 18 cm/7 in round Victoria Sandwich cakes (see basic recipe).

Blend the almond essence (extract) with the icing (frosting) mixture. Mix the cherries and nuts with one-third of the icing (frosting). Sandwich the cakes together with the nutty filling.

Dissolve the cocoa in the hot water, allow to cool and add to half of the remaining icing (frosting). Spread a little over the top of the cake and mark into squares. Using a very small fluted nozzle, pipe rosettes of icing (frosting) to fill in the squares, alternating white with chocolate.

Makes one 18 cm/7 in round cake

Lemon Mimosa Cake

METRIC/IMPERIAL
100 g/4 oz butter, softened
100 g/4 oz caster sugar
3 tablespoons lemon curd
grated rind of $\frac{1}{2}$ lemon
2 large eggs
225 g/8 oz self-raising flour, sifted
Filling:
4 tablespoons lemon curd
Icing and decoration:
100 g/4 oz icing sugar
lemon juice
10 mimosa balls
19 angelica leaves

AMERICAN
$\frac{1}{2}$ cup softened butter
$\frac{1}{2}$ cup sugar
3 tablespoons lemon curd
grated rind of $\frac{1}{2}$ lemon
2 large eggs
2 cups sifted self-rising flour
Filling:
4 tablespoons lemon curd
Frosting and decoration:
1 cup confectioners' sugar
lemon juice
10 mimosa balls
19 angelica leaves

Grease and line the base of an 18 cm/7 in cake tin (cake pan). Cream the butter and sugar until light and fluffy. Beat in the lemon curd and lemon rind, then gradually beat in the eggs.

Gradually fold the flour into the mixture until well mixed. Turn into the prepared cake tin (cake pan), level the surface and cook on the centre shelf of a preheated moderate oven (160°C/325°F, Gas Mark 3) for 55 minutes until a fine skewer inserted into the centre comes out clean. Allow to stand for 5 minutes before turning out on to a wire rack.

When cool, cut in half horizontally, fill with lemon curd and sandwich the two halves together.

Sift the icing sugar (confectioners' sugar) into a bowl, then add enough lemon juice to mix, keeping icing (frosting) fairly stiff. Spread over the cake. Place two mimosa balls and three angelica leaves at the centre of the cake. Round the edge of the cake, evenly space 8 more mimosa balls, each with an angelica leaf on either side.

Makes one 18 cm/7 in round cake

Sticky Devil Cake

METRIC/IMPERIAL	AMERICAN
150 g/5 oz plain flour	1¼ cups all-purpose flour
25 g/1 oz cornflour	¼ cup cornstarch
65 g/2½ oz cocoa powder	½ cup unsweetened cocoa
175 g/6 oz caster sugar	¾ cup sugar
¼ teaspoon bicarbonate of soda	¼ teaspoon baking soda
50 g/2 oz ground almonds	½ cup ground almonds
2 eggs	2 eggs
120 ml/4 fl oz pure corn oil	½ cup pure corn oil
175 ml/6 fl oz golden syrup	¾ cup maple syrup
175 ml/6 fl oz milk	¾ cup milk
Icing:	**Frosting:**
75 g/3 oz butter	⅓ cup butter
175 g/6 oz icing sugar, sifted	1⅓ cups sifted confectioners' sugar
1 egg yolk	1 egg yolk
100 g/4 oz plain chocolate, melted	4 squares semi-sweet chocolate, melted

Grease and line two 18 cm/7 in round cake tins (cake pans).

Sift together the flour, cornflour (cornstarch) cocoa, sugar and bicarbonate of soda (baking soda) and stir in the ground almonds. Mix together the eggs, corn oil, syrup and milk, add to the dry ingredients and beat well to form a smooth slack batter.

Divide the mixture between the prepared cake tins (cake pans) and bake in a preheated cool oven (150°C/300°F, Gas Mark 2) for 2 to 2¼ hours. Allow to cool slightly before turning out.

To make the icing (frosting), beat together the butter and icing sugar (confectioners' sugar) until light and creamy. Beat in the egg yolk and stir in the melted chocolate. Use half the icing (frosting) to sandwich the sponge cakes together and thickly coat the top of the cake with the remaining icing (frosting).

Makes one 18 cm/7 in round cake

STICKY DEVIL CAKE *(Photograph: Mazola Pure Corn Oil)*

CELEBRATION CAKES

Birthday Cake

METRIC/IMPERIAL
120 ml/4 fl oz corn oil
175 g/6 oz caster sugar
3 eggs, beaten
500 g/1 lb mixed dried fruit
50 g/2 oz chopped blanched almonds
50 g/2 oz glacé cherries
50 g/2 oz mixed peel
225 g/8 oz plain flour
1½ teaspoons baking powder
1 teaspoon mixed spice
2 to 3 tablespoons milk
apricot jam, warmed and sieved
1½ lb packet marzipan
Royal icing:
2 to 3 egg whites
500 g/1¼ lb icing sugar sifted
1 tablespoon lemon juice
2 teaspoons glycerine
To decorate:
icing flowers

AMERICAN
½ cup corn oil
¾ cup sugar
3 eggs, beaten
3 cups mixed dried fruit
½ cup chopped blanched almonds
¼ cup candied cherries
⅓ cup candied peel
2 cups all-purpose flour
1½ teaspoons baking powder
1 teaspoon mixed spice
2 to 3 tablespoons milk
apricot jam, warmed and sieved
1½ lb package marzipan
Royal icing:
2 to 3 egg whites
3½ cups sifted confectioners' sugar
1 tablespoon lemon juice
2 teaspoons glycerine
To decorate:
frosted flowers

Line a 20 cm/8 in round cake tin (cake pan) with a double layer of greaseproof paper (or non-stick parchment). Mix together the corn oil, sugar and eggs. Add the mixed dried fruit, almonds, glacé cherries (candied cherries) and mixed peel (candied peel) and beat well. Sift together the flour, baking powder and mixed spice and fold into the fruit batter. Add sufficient milk to form a soft dropping consistency. Place in the cake tin (cake pan) and bake in a preheated moderate oven (160°C/325°F, Gas Mark 3) for 2 to 2½ hours. Leave in the cake tin (cake pan) for 30 minutes, then turn out and cool on a wire rack.

Knead the marzipan until smooth. Dust a work top with caster sugar and roll out one third of the paste to a round large enough to cover the top of the cake. Brush the top of the cake with apricot jam, cover with marzipan and trim edges.

Roll out the remaining two thirds of the marzipan into a long strip, the length and width of the sides of the cake. Brush the sides with apricot jam and cover with marzipan, sealing the joins. Allow the marzipan to dry for at least four days before adding icing (frosting).

To make the icing (frosting) whisk the egg whites until frothy and add the sugar a little at a time. Beat until the icing (frosting) stands in peaks. Beat in the lemon juice and glycerine. Cover with a damp cloth to prevent hardening.

Transfer the cake to a board. Reserve a little of the icing (frosting) and spread the remainder over the cake, using a large flat-bladed knife (spatula) dipped in hot water. When icing (frosting) is set use the reserved icing (frosting) to pipe a shell edge around the base of the cake and fix the flowers in position.

Makes one 20 cm/8 in round cake

Henrietta Hedgehog

METRIC/IMPERIAL
175 g/6 oz margarine
175 g/6 oz caster sugar
3 eggs, beaten
150 g/5 oz self-raising flour
1 teaspoon baking powder
25 g/1 oz cocoa powder
To ice and decorate:
100 g/4 oz butter
175 g/6 oz icing sugar, sifted
1 tablespoon cocoa powder
2 packets chocolate buttons, halved
1 glacé cherry
2 roasted coffee beans **or** 2 seedless
    raisins

AMERICAN
$\frac{3}{4}$ cup margarine
$\frac{3}{4}$ cup sugar
3 eggs, beaten
$1\frac{1}{4}$ cups self-rising flour
1 teaspoon baking powder
$\frac{1}{4}$ cup unsweetened cocoa
To frost and decorate:
$\frac{1}{2}$ cup butter
$1\frac{1}{3}$ cups sifted confectioners' sugar
1 tablespoon unsweetened cocoa
2 packages chocolate buttons, halved
1 candied cherry
2 roasted coffee beans **or** 2 seedless
    raisins

Cream the margarine and sugar together until light and fluffy. Gradually beat in the eggs with a spoonful of flour. Sift the flour, baking powder and cocoa together and fold in. Add a little milk if the mixture (batter) is too dry. Turn into a 1.2 litre/2 pint/5 cup greased ovenproof basin and bake in a preheated oven (180°C/350°F, Gas Mark 4) for about one hour. Test by inserting a warm skewer into the centre of the cake; it will come out clean if the cake is cooked.

Make the icing (frosting) by beating together the butter and the icing sugar (confectioners' sugar). Dissolve the cocoa in a very little boiling water and mix into the butter icing (frosting).

Cut the cake in half vertically through the middle, and remove from the basin. Spread butter icing (frosting) over flat top end of each half and sandwich these together. Lift on to a plate or cake board and spread butter icing all over the cake. Put a little extra icing (frosting) at one end and form into a point for the 'snout'. Stick the halved chocolate buttons into the icing (frosting) at an angle to represent the spines, covering all the cake except the front part. Mark the 'face' with a fork and add the cherry for a 'nose' and coffee beans or raisins for the 'eyes'.

St. Valentine Gâteau

METRIC/IMPERIAL	AMERICAN
3 eggs	*3 eggs*
100 g/4 oz caster sugar	*$\frac{1}{2}$ cup sugar*
65 g/2$\frac{1}{2}$ oz plain flour	*$\frac{5}{8}$ cup all-purpose flour*
2 tablespoons cocoa powder	*2 tablespoons unsweetened cocoa*
Filling and decoration:	**Filling and decoration:**
300 ml/$\frac{1}{2}$ pint double cream	*1$\frac{1}{4}$ cups heavy cream*
few drops vanilla essence	*few drops vanilla extract*
225 g/8 oz milk chocolate	*8 squares chocolate*

Whisk the eggs and 75 g/3 oz/$\frac{1}{3}$ cup sugar in a bowl until pale and thick. Carefully fold in the flour and cocoa powder (unsweetened cocoa) with a metal spoon. Turn the mixture into two lightly greased and lined 20 cm/8 in heart-shaped tins. Bake in a moderately hot oven (190°C/375°F, Gas Mark 5) for 20 minutes. Cool.

Whip the double cream (heavy cream), vanilla essence (vanilla extract) and the remaining sugar together in a bowl. Sandwich the hearts together with about one third of the cream. Reserve 1 oz (1 square) of the chocolate, melt the remainder and use to coat the top and sides of the cake.

When the chocolate has set, decorate the top of the cake with the remaining whipped, piped cream and chocolate curls, made by slightly warming the remaining chocolate, then shaving off curls with a small, sharp knife or vegetable peeler.

Makes one heart-shaped cake

Wine Cake

METRIC/IMPERIAL	AMERICAN
150 g/5 oz sultanas	1 cup seedless white raisins
150 g/5 oz raisins	1 cup raisins
100 g/4 oz currants	$\frac{3}{4}$ cup currants
75 g/3 oz glacé cherries, quartered	$\frac{1}{3}$ cup quartered candied cherries
75 g/3 oz mixed, chopped peel	$\frac{1}{2}$ cup chopped candied peel
120 ml/4 fl oz sherry	$\frac{1}{2}$ cup sherry
150 g/5 oz butter	$\frac{5}{8}$ cup butter
150 g/5 oz soft brown sugar	$\frac{3}{4}$ cup light brown sugar
4 eggs	4 eggs
100 g/4 oz self-raising flour	1 cup self-rising flour
100 g/4 oz plain flour	1 cup all-purpose flour
pinch of salt	pinch of salt
$\frac{1}{2}$ teaspoon mixed spice	$\frac{1}{2}$ teaspoon mixed spice
25 g/1 oz ground almonds	$\frac{1}{4}$ cup ground almonds

Make this cake 6 to 8 weeks before it is required, and about a week before making it, mix together the washed and dried fruit, cherries and peel, then pour over the sherry and mix well. Leave to soak, stirring frequently and keep covered until needed.

Grease and line with a double thickness of greaseproof paper (non-stick parchment) a 20 cm/8 in round cake tin (pan). Cream together the butter and sugar until soft and fluffy. Gradually beat in the eggs. Fold in the flours, salt, spice and almonds. Drain off and keep the liquor from the fruit, then mix the fruit with the cake mixture (batter); stir well until blended.

Put into the prepared tin (pan), smooth the top and bake in a preheated moderate oven (160°C/325°F, Gas Mark 3) for one hour. Then cover the cake with foil, reduce the oven temperature to 150°C/300°F, Gas Mark 2 and cook for a further $1\frac{1}{2}$ hours until firm to the touch. Leave to stand in the tin (pan) until nearly cold.

Remove from the tin (pan), prick well and pour over the liquor from the dried fruit. Wrap the cake in foil or greaseproof paper and leave for 6 to 8 weeks to mature, before decorating as appropriate to the occasion, whether it be a birthday or other special anniversary.

Makes one 20 cm/8 in round cake

Rich Fruit Cake

(Basic all-in-one method)

METRIC/IMPERIAL

275 g/10 oz currants
200 g/7 oz sultanas
100 g/4 oz raisins
65 g/2½ oz glacé cherries, halved
65 g/2½ oz almonds, blanched and
  chopped
65 g/2½ oz mixed peel
grated rind of 1 lemon
200 g/7 oz plain flour, sifted
1 teaspoon mixed spice
1 teaspoon ground nutmeg
50 g/2 oz ground almonds
150 g/5 oz margarine
175 g/6 oz soft brown sugar
1 tablespoon black treacle
4 large eggs
2 tablespoons brandy (optional)

AMERICAN

2 cups currants
1¼ cups seedless white raisins
⅔ cup raisins
⅓ cup halved candied cherries
½ cup blanched and chopped almonds
⅓ cup candied peel
grated rind of 1 lemon
1¾ cups all-purpose flour
1 teaspoon mixed spice
1 teaspoon ground nutmeg
½ cup ground almonds
⅝ cup margarine
1 cup light brown sugar
1 tablespoon molasses
4 large eggs
2 tablespoons brandy (optional)

Line and grease the sides and bottom of a 20 cm/8 in round cake tin
(cake pan) or a 15 cm/7 in square cake tin (cake pan) with double
greaseproof paper, well greased (or non-stick parchment). Cut a double
strip of brown paper 2.5 cm/1 in higher than the depth of the tin (pan);
place it round the outside of the tin (pan) and secure with string. (This
prevents the cake from becoming too brown.)

Place all the cake ingredients except the brandy in a mixing bowl and
beat together with a wooden spoon for about 3 to 6 minutes until
well mixed. Place in the prepared tin (pan) and smooth the top with the
back of a wet metal spoon. Bake in the middle of a preheated cool oven
(140°C/275°F, Gas Mark 1) for 3 hours, then test. If cooked, the cake
should spring back when gently pressed with the fingers. It should be
evenly risen and beginning to shrink from the sides of the tin (pan) and
should have stopped bubbling. If not cooked, continue cooking and test
every 30 minutes.

When cooked, allow to cool in the tin (pan). When cold, remove
from the tin (pan); if brandy is to be added lightly prick the base of the
cake and spoon brandy over it. This helps to keep the cake moist. Wrap
in foil and store in a cool place. (Rich fruit cakes need to be made two
months before they are required, to allow the flavour to mature and
develop.)

Makes one 20 cm/8 in round cake or one 15 cm/7 in square cake

Simnel Cake

METRIC/IMPERIAL
1½ lb packet marzipan
Cake:
225 g/8 oz margarine
225 g/8 oz caster sugar
50 g/2 oz ground almonds
4 large eggs
350 g/12 oz plain flour, sifted
½ teaspoon ground nutmeg
350 g/12 oz currants
225 g/8 oz raisins
225 g/8 oz sultanas
100 g/4 oz mixed peel
½ wine glass brandy
Icing:
100 g/4 oz icing sugar
1 to 2 tablespoons water
apricot jam, sieved
a little beaten egg white

AMERICAN
1½ lb package marzipan
Cake:
1 cup margarine
1 cup firmly packed sugar
½ cup ground almonds
4 large eggs
3 cups all-purpose flour, sifted
½ teaspoon ground nutmeg
2 cups currants
1½ cups raisins
1½ cups seedless white raisins
⅔ cup candied peel
½ wine glass brandy
Frosting:
1 cup confectioners' sugar
1 to 2 tablespoons water
apricot jam, strained
a little egg white, beaten

Line a 23 cm/9 in round cake tin (cake pan) with greaseproof paper (or non-stick parchment).

Knead the marzipan well and divide into three. Roll one-third into a 23 cm/9 in round and reserve the remaining two-thirds.

To make the cake, cream the margarine and sugar in a bowl until light and fluffy, add the almonds and 3 eggs, gradually, beating well. Add 2 tablespoons of the flour, the nutmeg and remaining egg, beating well. Add the fruit, mixed peel (candied peel) and brandy and then fold in remaining flour. Place half the mixture (batter) into the prepared tin (pan). Cover with the round of almond paste and place the remaining cake mixture (batter) on top. Smooth over the surface. Bake in a moderate oven (180°C/350°F, Gas Mark 4) for 1 hour, then reduce the heat to cool (150°C/300°F, Gas Mark 2) for a further 2½ hours. Leave to cool.

To make the icing (frosting), beat the icing sugar (confectioners' sugar) and water together until smooth and glossy. Ice (frost) the top of the cake, leaving a 1 cm/½ in border round the edge. Brush this border with jam. Shape a 2.5 cm/1 in ring of marzipan to fit the outer border of the cake. Place in position. Shape the remaining marzipan into 11 balls, brush with egg white, and place under a hot grill until lightly browned. Arrange, evenly spaced, around the border of the cake.
Makes one 23 cm/9 in round cake

SIMNEL CAKE, HOT CROSS BUNS *(page 74)*, EASTER BISCUITS
(page 60) (Photograph: Kraft Foods Ltd)

Christmas Rose Cake

METRIC/IMPERIAL

1 × 20 cm/8 in round basic rich fruit
  cake mixture (see page 39)
apricot jam, warmed and sieved

Almond paste:
500 g/1 lb ground almonds
225 g/8 oz icing sugar, sifted
225 g/8 oz caster sugar
4 egg yolks
½ teaspoon almond essence
1 teaspoon lemon juice

Fondant icing:
500 g/1 lb icing sugar, sifted
1 egg white
1 tablespoon liquid glucose, warmed
a little cornflour

Royal icing:
1 egg white
225 g/8 oz icing sugar, sifted

To decorate:
2 metres/2 yards red satin ribbon
holly leaves

AMERICAN

1 × 8 in round basic rich fruit cake
  batter (see page 39)
apricot jam, warmed and strained

Almond paste:
4 cups ground almonds
2 cups sifted confectioners' sugar
1 cup firmly packed sugar
4 egg yolks
½ teaspoon almond extract
1 teaspoon lemon juice

Fondant frosting:
3½ cups sifted confectioners' sugar
1 egg white
1 tablespoon liquid glucose, warmed
cornstarch

Royal frosting:
1 egg white
2 cups sifted confectioners' sugar

To decorate:
2 yards red satin ribbon
holly leaves

Make up the cake mixture (batter) and bake as for basic recipe.

To make the almond paste, mix the almonds and sugars together. Beat the egg yolks with the almond essence (extract) and lemon juice. Stir into the almond mixture and mix to a firm paste.

Brush the top and sides of the cake with the apricot jam, and cover with the almond paste. Put the cake on a cake board, smooth any joins and leave for a day before icing (frosting).

To make the fondant icing (frosting), put into a bowl the egg white, sugar and glucose. Blend together with a palette knife until evenly mixed, then knead firmly together with the finger tips on a work surface dusted with icing sugar (confectioners' sugar) until soft, pliable and easy to handle.

Roll out the icing (frosting) 5 cm/2 in larger all round than the top of the cake. Brush the almond paste with egg white, then dip fingers in cornflour (cornstarch) and place the icing (frosting) on top of the cake. Mould until the cake is completely covered.

To make the Royal icing (frosting), lightly whisk the egg white until foamy, beat in the sugar a little at a time, using a wooden spoon, until the Royal icing (frosting) stands up in stiff peaks when the spoon is removed.

To decorate, using a fluted nozzle and half the Royal icing (frosting), pipe a scroll around the bottom of the cake. With the remaining icing (frosting), using a petal nozzle, pipe the Christmas roses and leave to dry separately.

Lay two bands of red ribbon diagonally across the cake; secure the roses and holly leaves with a spot of Royal icing (frosting). With a thin writing nozzle, pipe 'Christmas Greetings'.

Makes one 20 cm/8 in round cake

Christmas Kringle

METRIC/IMPERIAL
75 g/3 oz butter
2 tablespoons sugar
4 tablespoons milk, warmed
2 teaspoons dried yeast
1 egg, beaten
225 g/8 oz strong plain flour
Filling:
50 g/2 oz butter, softened
50 g/2 oz sugar
2 teaspoons ground cinnamon
To decorate:
a little beaten egg
25 g/1 oz chopped blanched almonds
25 g/1 oz sugar
glacé icing (optional)

AMERICAN
⅓ cup butter
2 tablespoons sugar
4 tablespoons milk, warmed
2 teaspoons active dry yeast
1 egg, beaten
2 cups all-purpose flour
Filling:
¼ cup butter, softened
¼ cup sugar
2 teaspoons ground cinnamon
To decorate:
a little beaten egg
¼ cup chopped blanched almonds
2 teaspoons firmly packed sugar
glacé frosting (optional)

Melt the butter and set aside until tepid. In a large bowl dissolve $\frac{1}{2}$ teaspoon sugar in the warmed milk, sprinkle on the yeast and whisk well; leave until frothy. Stir the remaining sugar, beaten egg and melted, cooled butter into the yeast liquid. Beat in the flour gradually until a dough is formed. Knead until smooth on a lightly floured surface. Place in a greased polythene (plastic) bag and leave to rise in a warm place until double in size, about 30 to 40 minutes.

Cream together the filling ingredients.

Knock back (punch down) the dough and roll to a thin strip 80 cm/32 in long and 12.5 cm/5 in wide. Spread the filling along the middle and fold the sides over to enclose it. Fold into three and place the long strip on a greased baking sheet. Shape into a pretzel by folding the dough round into an oval, crossing over the ends. The dough ends should just touch the inner back edge of the oval. Cover with greased polythene (plastic). Leave to rise for about 15 minutes.

Brush with beaten egg, sprinkle with the almonds and sugar. Bake in a preheated moderately hot oven (200°C/400°F, Gas Mark 6) for 20 minutes until golden. When cool, decorate with glacé icing (frosting) if liked.

Christmas Igloo Cake

METRIC/IMPERIAL
175 g/6 oz butter
75 g/3 oz caster sugar
3 tablespoons thick honey
3 eggs
250 g/9 oz self-raising flour
6 tablespoons milk
Filling:
50 g/2 oz softened butter
1 tablespoon thick honey
50 g/2 oz icing sugar
grated rind of 1 orange
To decorate:
a little clear honey
750 g/1½ lb marzipan
500 g/1 lb icing sugar
1 egg white
75 g/3 oz chocolate drops
Christmas cake decorations –
  Christmas trees, snowmen, skiers,
  etc.

AMERICAN
¾ cup butter
6 tablespoons firmly packed sugar
3 tablespoons thick honey
3 eggs
2¼ cups self-rising flour
6 tablespoons milk
Filling:
¼ cup softened butter
1 tablespoon thick honey
½ cup confectioners' sugar
grated rind of 1 orange
To decorate:
a little clear honey
1½ lb marzipan
4 cups confectioners' sugar
1 egg white
½ cup chocolate buttons
Christmas cake decorations –
  Christmas trees, snowmen, skiers,
  etc.

Grease and line a deep 20 cm/8 in cake tin (cake pan). Put the butter, sugar and honey in a mixing bowl and beat together until creamy. Whisk the eggs and gradually beat into the mixture, adding a little of the flour. Finally fold in the rest of the flour and the milk. Turn the mixture into the tin (pan) and bake in a preheated moderate oven (180°C/350°F, Gas Mark 4) for 45 to 50 minutes. Turn out to cool.

Mix the filling ingredients together to form a smooth cream. Cut the cake in half horizontally and sandwich with the cream.

Spread a little clear honey over the top and sides of the cake. Using about a third of the marzipan, make a dome shape on the top of the cake. Roll out another third of the marzipan into a round to fit over the top of the cake. Roll the rest of the marzipan into an oblong about 12 cm/5 in wide. Divide in half lengthwise and use to cover the sides of the cake. Press on well and trim off any remaining marzipan.

Sift the icing sugar (confectioners' sugar) into a bowl. Add the lightly beaten egg white and mix to a stiff paste using a wooden spoon. Use a palette or table knife (dipping it occasionally in hot water) to spread the icing over the cake. Leave to set. When firm, melt the chocolate and when cool, pipe lines around the cake to resemble the ice-block shapes of an igloo.

Carefully transfer the igloo cake to a serving plate and add Christmas decorations as required.

Makes one 20 cm/8 in cake

CHRISTMAS IGLOO CAKE *(Photograph: Gale's Honey)*

SMALL CAKES AND BISCUITS (COOKIES)

Cream Horns

METRIC/IMPERIAL
350 g/12 oz packet puff pastry
1 egg, beaten
3 tablespoons sugar
100 g/4 oz jam
Filling:
300 ml/½ pint double cream
1 teaspoon vanilla essence
1 tablespoon icing sugar
2 tablespoons milk
To decorate:
12 strawberries

AMERICAN
¾ lb package puff paste
1 egg, beaten
3 tablespoons sugar
⅓ cup preserve
Filling:
1¼ cups heavy cream
1 teaspoon vanilla extract
1 tablespoon confectioners' sugar
2 tablespoons milk
To decorate:
12 strawberries

Roll out the dough to about .75 cm/¼ in thick. Cut into 12 long strips, about 2.5 cm/1 in wide. Brush one side of each strip with water and carefully wind round the outside of 12 greased cream horn tins (metal cones), overlapping slightly so that there are no gaps. Transfer the tins (cones) to a damp baking sheet, brush with the beaten egg and sprinkle the sugar over. Set aside for 30 minutes.

Place in a preheated very hot oven (230°C/450°F, Gas Mark 8) and bake for 20 to 25 minutes, or until golden brown. Gently transfer to a wire rack to cool.

When cold, remove the tins from the pastry. Put a tablespoonful of jam into the bottom of the horns. Beat the filling ingredients together until thick, then spoon into the horns. Top each cream horn with a strawberry.
Makes 12 horns

Chocolate Truffle Squares

METRIC/IMPERIAL

Base:

75 g/3 oz plain flour

25 g/1 oz cornflour

½ teaspoon salt

50 g/2 oz butter

25 g/1 oz caster sugar

1 tablespoon water

Filling:

225 g/8 oz digestive biscuits, crushed

75 g/3 oz icing sugar

25 g/1 oz glacé cherries, chopped

25 g/1 oz mixed peel

25 g/1 oz mixed dried fruit

2 tablespoons cocoa powder

6 tablespoons water

Topping:

100 g/4 oz plain chocolate

1 teaspoon pure corn oil

AMERICAN

Base:

¾ cup all-purpose flour

¼ cup cornstarch

½ teaspoon salt

¼ cup butter

2 tablespoons firmly packed sugar

1 tablespoon water

Filling:

2 cups crushed Graham crackers

¾ cup confectioners' sugar

3 tablespoons chopped candied cherries

3 tablespoons candied peel

3 tablespoons mixed dried fruit

2 tablespoons unsweetened cocoa

6 tablespoons water

Topping:

4 squares semi-sweet chocolate

1 teaspoon pure corn oil

To make the base, sift together the flour, cornflour (cornstarch) and salt and rub in the butter. Stir in the sugar and water and mix to a firm dough. Transfer to a lightly floured board, roll out to 18 cm/7 in square. Place the dough on a baking sheet, prick and bake in a preheated moderately hot oven (200°C/400°F, Gas Mark 6) for 20 minutes.

To make the filling, mix together the biscuits (Graham crackers), icing sugar (confectioners' sugar), cherries, cut peel and dried fruit. Blend the cocoa with the water in a saucepan and bring to the boil, stirring continuously. Add to the dry ingredients, mix well and spread over the cooked pastry base.

To make the topping, melt the chocolate in a small bowl over a pan of hot water, add the oil and mix well. Spread the filling over the base and make a rippled effect with a fork. Leave to set in the refrigerator, then cut into squares.

Makes 16 small squares

Polkas

METRIC/IMPERIAL

Choux pastry:
50 g/2 oz butter
150 ml/$\frac{1}{4}$ pint water
65 g/2$\frac{1}{2}$ oz plain flour, sifted
pinch of salt
2 eggs
8 digestive biscuits

Filling and decoration:
2 to 4 teaspoons warm water **or**
  orange or lemon juice
orange or lemon colouring (optional)
100 g/4 oz icing sugar, sifted
1 × 225 g/8 oz can fruit cocktail
  drained
150 ml/$\frac{1}{4}$ pint double cream, whipped

AMERICAN

Choux pastry:
$\frac{1}{4}$ cup butter
$\frac{2}{3}$ cup water
$\frac{5}{8}$ cup sifted all-purpose flour
pinch of salt
2 eggs
8 Graham crackers

Filling and decoration:
2 to 4 teaspoons warm water **or**
  orange or lemon juice
orange or lemon coloring (optional)
1 cup sifted confectioners' sugar
1 × $\frac{1}{2}$ lb can fruit cocktail, drained
$\frac{2}{3}$ cup heavy cream, whipped

To make the choux pastry, melt the butter in the water in a saucepan. Bring to the boil and remove from the heat immediately. Beat in the flour and salt, using a wooden spoon, over a low heat until a soft ball forms and the mixture leaves the sides of the saucepan. Cool slightly, then beat in the eggs one at a time until completely absorbed and the mixture is smooth and shiny.

Place the digestive biscuits (Graham crackers) on a baking sheet. Pipe the choux paste through a 1 cm/$\frac{1}{2}$ in plain nozzle round the edge of each biscuit (cracker). Bake above the middle of a preheated moderately hot oven (200°C/400°F, Gas Mark 6) for 15 minutes. Then turn down the heat to 190°C/375°F, Gas Mark 5 for 6 to 10 minutes until the pastry is well risen and golden brown. Cool on a wire rack.

To make the icing (frosting) stir the water or orange or lemon juice into the icing sugar (confectioners' sugar) and the colouring, if used. Dip the choux tops into the icing (frosting) to coat them. Stand them upright on a wire rack. Fill with the fruit and decorate with the cream just before serving.

Makes 8 small cakes

POLKAS (Photograph: British Egg Information Service)

Honey Squares

METRIC/IMPERIAL	AMERICAN
100 g/4 oz plain flour	1 cup all-purpose flour
1 teaspoon cinnamon	1 teaspoon cinnamon
1 teaspoon ginger	1 teaspoon ginger
$\frac{1}{2}$ teaspoon bicarbonate of soda	$\frac{1}{2}$ teaspoon baking soda
$\frac{1}{4}$ teaspoon salt	$\frac{1}{4}$ teaspoon salt
3 tablespoons oil	3 tablespoons oil
3 tablespoons honey	3 tablespoons honey
3 tablespoons black treacle	3 tablespoons molasses
50 g/2 oz demerara sugar	$\frac{1}{3}$ cup light brown sugar
1 egg beaten up with 2 tablespoons milk	1 egg beaten up with 2 tablespoons milk
50 g/2 oz sultanas (optional)	$\frac{1}{3}$ cup seedless white raisins (optional)
Topping:	**Topping:**
chopped walnuts or flaked almonds	chopped walnuts or slivered almonds

Sift the flour, spices, bicarbonate of soda (baking soda), and salt into a bowl and mix together. Add the remaining ingredients, including the sultanas (seedless white raisins) if desired, and quickly beat all together until the mixture is smooth. Grease and line an 18 cm/7 in square tin (pan) and pour in the cake mixture (cake batter).

Sprinkle a few chopped walnuts or flaked (slivered) almonds over the top and bake in a preheated moderate oven (180°C/350°F, Gas Mark 4) for 30 minutes until firm. Cool on a wire rack, then cut into squares.
Makes 9 square cakes

Madeleines

METRIC/IMPERIAL	AMERICAN
75 g/3 oz plain flour, sifted	$\frac{3}{4}$ cup all-purpose flour, sifted
3 eggs, separated	3 eggs, separated
75 g/3 oz caster sugar	$\frac{1}{3}$ cup sugar
To decorate:	**To decorate:**
warmed and sieved jam	warmed and strained preserve
desiccated coconut	shredded coconut
8 glacé cherries	8 candied cherries

Put the flour into a bowl and leave it in a warm place until needed. Whisk the egg whites until stiff. Beat in the sugar, a little at a time, alternately with the egg yolks until all the sugar and yolks are whisked in. Carefully fold in the flour.

Three parts fill 15 greased and floured dariole moulds (molds) and bake in the middle of a preheated, moderately hot oven (190°C/375°F,

Gas Mark 5) for 15 to 20 minutes. Cool on a wire rack. Cut a slice from the broad ends so the cakes stand level. Brush them with the jam (preserve) and roll them in coconut. Top each with half a glacé cherry (candied cherry).
Makes 15 small cakes

Coffee Eclairs

METRIC/IMPERIAL
Choux pastry:
50 g/2 oz butter
150 ml/¼ pint water
65 g/2½ oz plain flour
small pinch of salt
2 eggs
Filling:
150 ml/5 fl oz double cream, stiffly
  whipped
2 tablespoons caster sugar
2 tablespoons milk
Icing:
250 g/9 oz icing sugar, sifted
3 tablespoons strong black coffee

AMERICAN
Choux pastry:
¼ cup butter
⅔ cup water
⅝ cup all-purpose flour
small pinch of salt
2 eggs
Filling:
⅔ cup heavy cream, stiffly whipped
2 tablespoons sugar
2 tablespoons milk
Frosting:
2 cups sifted confectioners' sugar
3 tablespoons strong black coffee

To make the choux pastry, melt the butter in the water in a saucepan and bring to the boil. Remove from the heat immediately and beat in the flour and salt with a wooden spoon until the dough is smooth. Return to a low heat and continue to beat until the dough forms a ball and leaves the sides of the pan clean. Cool the dough slightly and beat in the eggs, one at a time, until completely absorbed and the mixture is smooth and shiny.

Spoon the pastry dough into a piping (pastry) bag with a plain tube nozzle. Pipe 5 cm/2 in lengths of dough on to well-greased baking sheets. Bake in a preheated moderately hot oven (200°C/400°F, Gas Mark 6) for 10 minutes. Reduce the oven temperature to moderate (180°C/350°F, Gas Mark 4) and continue to bake for 20 to 25 minutes, or until the éclairs are puffed up and golden brown.

Make a slit in the side of each éclair and, using a teaspoon, carefully scoop out any soft dough from inside. Return to the oven for 5 minutes to dry out. Cool on a wire rack.

To make the filling, beat all the ingredients together until the mixture is very thick. Slice the éclairs in half lengthways and fill generously with the filling.

To make the icing (frosting), mix together the icing sugar (confectioners' sugar) and coffee. Dip the tops of the éclairs in the icing (frosting), or spread it with a knife.
Makes about 10 éclairs

Fruity Cream Eclairs

METRIC/IMPERIAL
Choux pastry:
65 g/2½ oz plain flour
15 g/½ oz cornflour
2 teaspoons caster sugar
pinch of salt
5 tablespoons pure corn oil
150 ml/¼ pint water
2 eggs
Filling:
225 g/8 oz fresh fruit – raspberries,
  strawberries, peaches or
  blackcurrants
2 tablespoons caster sugar
150 ml/5 fl oz double cream,
  whipped
sifted icing sugar for dusting

AMERICAN
Choux pastry:
⅝ cup all-purpose flour
2 tablespoons cornstarch
2 teaspoons sugar
pinch of salt
5 tablespoons pure corn oil
⅔ cup water
2 eggs
Filling:
½ lb fresh fruit – raspberries,
  strawberries, peaches or
  blackcurrants
2 tablespoons sugar
⅔ cup heavy cream, whipped
sifted confectioners' sugar for dusting

Sift together the flour, cornflour (cornstarch), sugar and salt. Heat the oil and water to boiling point and add to the dry ingredients. Beat well until the mixture leaves the sides of the bowl. Allow to cool slightly, then beat in the eggs one at a time.

Spoon the pastry dough into a piping (pastry) bag and using a plain nozzle, pipe fingers on to a greased baking sheet. Bake in a preheated hot oven (220°C/425°F, Gas Mark 7) for 25 minutes. Cool on a wire rack and slit along one side.

To make the filling, liquidize or sieve (strain) the fruit with the sugar to form a purée (paste). Fold in the whipped cream and use to fill the éclairs. Dust the tops with icing sugar (confectioners' sugar) before serving.

Makes 10 to 12 éclairs

FRUITY CREAM ECLAIRS (Photograph: Mazola Pure Corn Oil)

Ginger Nuts

(Basic Recipe)

METRIC/IMPERIAL	AMERICAN
100 g/4 oz self-raising flour	*1 cup self-rising flour*
2 teaspoons caster sugar	*2 teaspoons sugar*
$\frac{1}{2}$ teaspoon bicarbonate of soda	*$\frac{1}{2}$ teaspoon baking soda*
1 to 2 teaspoons ground ginger	*1 to 2 teaspoons ground ginger*
1 teaspoon ground cinnamon	*1 teaspoon ground cinnamon*
50 g/2 oz butter	*$\frac{1}{4}$ cup butter*
75 g/3 oz golden syrup	*$\frac{1}{4}$ cup maple syrup*

Sift all the dry ingredients together in a bowl. Place the butter and golden syrup (maple syrup) in a saucepan and warm over a low heat, stirring until the butter has melted. Do not let the mixture boil. Remove from the heat and pour on to the dry ingredients. Stir well with a wooden spoon until smooth. Leave mixture to cool for a short time so that it becomes firm.

Makes one quantity basic Ginger Nut mixture.

Ginger Nut Men

METRIC/IMPERIAL	AMERICAN
1 quantity basic ginger nut mixture *(see above)*	*1 quantity basic ginger nut mixture* *(see above)*
currants for eyes	*currants for eyes*
Icing:	**Frosting:**
100 g/4 oz icing sugar	*1 cup confectioners' sugar*
2 tablespoons water	*2 tablespoons water*

Make up the basic mixture and chill until cold and firm. Roll out on a lightly floured surface to 3 mm/$\frac{1}{8}$ in thick. With a 'gingerbread man' cutter, stamp out the biscuits (cookies) or cut round a cardboard shape using a sharp knife. Carefully lift the biscuits (cookies) on to greased baking sheets, allowing room for spreading. Decorate with currants for eyes.

Bake just above the centre of a preheated moderately hot oven (190°C/375°F, Gas Mark 5) for about 15 minutes. Cool on baking sheets for a few minutes, then lift carefully on to a wire rack to cool.

To make the icing (frosting) put the icing sugar (confectioners' sugar) in a bowl and mix to a stiff paste with the water. Use for decoration of bows and buttons.

Makes about 10

Ginger Garlands

METRIC/IMPERIAL
1 quantity basic ginger nut mixture
 (see page 54)
To decorate:
angelica
glacé cherries
silver balls

AMERICAN
1 quantity basic ginger nut mixture
 (see page 54)
To decorate:
angelica
candied cherries
silver balls

Make up the basic mixture and chill until firm.

With lightly floured hands, roll the mixture into small pea-sized balls. Arrange on greased baking sheets in circles of 8 to 9 balls, almost touching but leaving space between the garlands for spreading. Decorate each ball with a small piece of angelica or glacé cherry (candied cherry) or a silver ball.

Bake just above the centre of a preheated moderately hot oven (190°C/375°F, Gas Mark 5) for about 10 minutes. Cool on the baking sheets for a few minutes, then lift carefully on to a wire rack to cool.
Makes about 20 to 30

Hazel Nutties

METRIC/IMPERIAL
100 g/4 oz hazelnuts
100 g/4 oz demerara sugar
about $\frac{1}{2}$ egg, beaten

AMERICAN
$\frac{3}{4}$ cup hazelnuts
$\frac{2}{3}$ cup light brown sugar
about $\frac{1}{2}$ egg, beaten

Line one or two baking sheets with non-stick parchment. Toast the hazelnuts under a moderate grill (broiler) until the skins split and the nuts brown. Cool slightly, then rub off the skins. Grind the nuts and put into a bowl with the sugar. Mix well and bind to a pliable dough with the egg.

Turn onto a sheet of non-stick parchment or an oiled board. Using an oiled rolling pin, roll out to about 3mm/$\frac{1}{8}$ in thick. Cut into 4 cm/$1\frac{1}{2}$ in plain rounds and transfer carefully to the lined baking sheets. Bake in a moderate oven (180°C/350°F, Gas Mark 4) for 10 to 12 minutes or until golden brown. Cool slightly, then remove carefully to a wire rack to cool.
Makes 20 to 24

Brandy Snaps

METRIC/IMPERIAL
50 g/2 oz margarine
50 g/2 oz demerara sugar
3 tablespoons golden syrup
50 g/2 oz plain flour
1 teaspoon ground ginger
½ teaspoon lemon juice
Filling:
150 ml/5 fl oz double cream,
  whipped

AMERICAN
¼ cup margarine
⅓ cup light brown sugar
3 tablespoons maple syrup
½ cup all-purpose flour
1 teaspoon ground ginger
½ teaspoon lemon juice
Filling:
⅔ cup heavy cream, whipped

Place the margarine, sugar and golden syrup (maple syrup) in a saucepan and melt over a low heat. Do not boil. Sift together the flour and ginger. Stir into the mixture with the lemon juice. Place heaped teaspoons of the mixture on greased baking sheets. Bake on the second and third shelves from the top of a preheated moderate oven (180°C/350°F, Gas Mark 4) for 15 to 20 minutes.

When cooked (but still soft) *allow to stand for 1 minute*. Lift from the baking sheets with a palette knife and roll round greased wooden spoon handles. When set, remove from wooden spoons and cool on a wire rack. Fill with whipped cream just before serving.
Makes 12

From top clockwise: WELSH CAKES *(page 59)*, CHOCOLATE FEATHER CAKE *(page 26)*, DEVONSHIRE SPLITS *(page 75)*, SHORTBREAD *(page 58)*, BRANDY SNAPS, BANANA AND NUT TEABREAD *(page 62) (Photograph: Stork Cookery Service)*

Shortbread

METRIC/IMPERIAL
175 g/6 oz plain flour
50 g/2 oz caster sugar
100 g/4 oz butter or margarine
To decorate:
caster sugar

AMERICAN
1½ cups all-purpose flour
¼ cup sugar
½ cup butter or margarine
To decorate:
sugar

Place the flour and sugar in a bowl and rub in the fat until the mixture resembles fine breadcrumbs. Knead together to form a smooth dough which leaves the sides of the bowl clean. Turn out on to a lightly floured surface and knead until dough becomes smooth and silky.

Press into a shortbread mould (mold) or a 20 cm/8 in round sandwich tin (layer cake pan), and smooth the top. Turn out on to a baking sheet. If a sandwich tin (layer cake pan) is used, flute the edges by pressing with the thumb all round. Prick all over with a fork. Mark into 7 portions.

Bake in a preheated cool oven (150°C/300°F, Gas Mark 2) for 50 to 60 minutes. Sprinkle with sugar.
Makes one 20 cm/8 in round shortbread or 7 biscuits (cookies).

Florentines

METRIC/IMPERIAL
50 g/2 oz butter
50 g/2 oz sugar
50 g/2 oz walnuts, finely chopped
15 g/½ oz chopped mixed peel
15 g/½ oz chopped glacé cherries
15 g/½ oz sultanas
1 tablespoon single cream
To decorate:
75 g/3 oz plain chocolate

AMERICAN
¼ cup butter
¼ cup sugar
½ cup finely chopped walnuts
1½ tablespoons chopped candied peel
2 tablespoons chopped candied cherries
1½ tablespoons seedless white raisins
1 tablespoon light cream
To decorate:
3 squares semi-sweet chocolate

Melt the butter in a saucepan. Add the sugar and stir until it has dissolved. Add all the remaining ingredients, except the chocolate, and beat well. Drop teaspoons of the batter, well spaced apart on to well-greased baking sheets. Place in a preheated moderate oven (180°C/350°F, Gas Mark 4) for 10 minutes or until golden brown. Remove from the oven and quickly press into neat circles with a palette knife. Cool slightly, then transfer to a wire rack to cool completely.

Melt the chocolate and spread over the backs of the biscuits and mark with a fork in a wavy pattern. Leave to set before serving.
Makes about 20 biscuits

Welsh Cakes

METRIC/IMPERIAL	AMERICAN
225 g/8 oz self-raising flour	2 cups self-rising flour
$\frac{1}{4}$ teaspoon salt	$\frac{1}{4}$ teaspoon salt
$\frac{1}{2}$ teaspoon mixed spice	$\frac{1}{2}$ teaspoon mixed spice
75 g/3 oz margarine	$\frac{1}{3}$ cup margarine
50 g/2 oz caster sugar	$\frac{1}{4}$ cup sugar
50 g/2 oz currants	6 tablespoons currants
1 egg, beaten	1 egg, beaten
1 tablespoon milk	1 tablespoon milk

Sift together the flour, salt and spice. Rub the margarine into the sifted ingredients until the mixture resembles fine breadcrumbs. Mix in the sugar and currants. Add the egg and milk to the mixture and bind to make a fairly firm dough. Turn out on to a floured surface and knead lightly. Roll out to a thickness of about 6 mm/$\frac{1}{4}$ in. Cut into rounds, using a 6 cm or 6.5 cm/2 or $2\frac{1}{2}$ in plain or fluted cutter.

Bake on a hot griddle or frying pan (skillet), greased with cooking fat, for 2 to 3 minutes on each side until golden brown. Serve hot.

Makes about 12 to 14 small cakes

Coffee Nut Cookies

METRIC/IMPERIAL	AMERICAN
50 g/2 oz butter	$\frac{1}{4}$ cup butter
75 g/3 oz caster sugar	$\frac{1}{3}$ cup sugar
75 g/3 oz cooked sieved potatoes	$\frac{1}{3}$ cup cooked strained potatoes
1 egg	1 egg
100 g/4 oz self-raising flour	1 cup self-rising flour
50 g/2 oz desiccated coconut	$\frac{2}{3}$ cup shredded coconut
1 tablespoon liquid coffee	1 tablespoon liquid coffee

Cream together the butter and sugar. Add the potatoes, then beat in the egg. Stir in the flour, coconut and coffee and mix well together. Place small spoonfuls on a greased baking sheet and bake in a preheated moderately hot oven (200°C/400°F, Gas Mark 6) for 10 to 15 minutes.

Makes 12 cookies

Vanilla Butter Biscuits (Cookies)

METRIC/IMPERIAL
225 g/8 oz butter
175 g/6 oz caster sugar
350 g/12 oz plain flour
1 teaspoon baking powder
pinch of salt
2 teaspoons vanilla essence
sifted icing sugar

AMERICAN
1 cup butter
$\frac{3}{4}$ cup sugar
3 cups all-purpose flour
1 teaspoon baking powder
pinch of salt
2 teaspoons vanilla extract
sifted confectioners' sugar

In a bowl, work the butter with a wooden spoon to soften it a little, then knead in the remaining ingredients. Knead well together and form into two neat rolls about 5 cm/2 in in diameter. Roll up carefully in two pieces of foil and chill for about 1 hour, or until required.

With a sharp knife slice off 40 6 mm/$\frac{1}{4}$ in slices and arrange them well apart on lightly greased baking sheets. Bake near the top of a preheated moderately hot oven (190°C/375°F. Gas Mark 5) for 15 minutes until lightly browned. Allow to cool on the baking sheets before placing them on cooling racks. When cold, dust with icing (confectioners') sugar.
Makes about 40 round biscuits (cookies)

Easter Biscuits (Cookies)

METRIC/IMPERIAL
100 g/4 oz soft margarine
100 g/4 oz caster sugar
1 egg yolk
225 g/8 oz plain flour
$\frac{1}{2}$ teaspoon ground cinnamon
50 g/2 oz currants
caster sugar

AMERICAN
$\frac{1}{2}$ cup soft margarine
$\frac{1}{2}$ cup sugar
1 egg yolk
2 cups all-purpose flour
$\frac{1}{2}$ teaspoon ground cinnamon
6 tablespoons currants
sugar

Cream the margarine and sugar until pale and fluffy; beat in the egg yolk. Sift together the flour and cinnamon and fold into the creamed mixture. Stir in the currants. Gather the mixture together into a dough, turn on to a floured board and knead lightly to remove any cracks.

Roll out the dough to 6 mm/$\frac{1}{4}$ in thick and cut into rounds with a 7.5 cm/3 in fluted cutter. Lift carefully on to a greased baking sheet with a palette knife and prick with a fork. Bake in a preheated moderate oven (180°C/350°F. Gas Mark 4) for 10 to 15 minutes, until pale golden, then lift on to a rack to cool. When cold, dust with sugar.
Makes about 12 biscuits

HONEY SQUARES *(page 50)* *(Photograph: Gale's Honey)*

TEABREADS, SCONES AND BUNS

Banana and Nut Teabread

METRIC/IMPERIAL
100 g/4 oz margarine
50 g/2 oz glacé cherries, halved
25 g/1 oz walnuts, chopped
100 g/4 oz sultanas
50 g/2 oz mixed peel
3 to 4 bananas, mashed
225 g/8 oz self-raising flour, sifted
175 g/6 oz caster sugar
2 eggs
To decorate:
100 g/4 oz icing sugar, sifted
1 to 1½ tablespoons warm water
glacé cherry halves
walnut halves

AMERICAN
½ cup margarine
¼ cup halved candied cherries
¼ cup chopped walnuts
⅔ cup seedless white raisins
6 tablespoons candied peel
3 to 4 bananas, mashed
2 cups self-rising flour, sifted
¾ cup sugar
2 eggs
To decorate:
1 cup sifted confectioners' sugar
1 to 1½ tablespoons warm water
candied cherry halves
walnut halves

Place all the cake ingredients in a mixing bowl and beat with a wooden spoon until well mixed, two to three minutes. Place the mixture (batter) in a greased and bottom-lined 1 kg/2 lb loaf tin (loaf pan) and bake in the centre of a preheated moderate oven (190°C/375°F, Gas Mark 5) for 1¾ to 2¼ hours. Leave to cool slightly before turning out.

To make the glacé icing (frosting), place icing sugar (confectioners' sugar) in a bowl with the water and beat with a wooden spoon until smooth. When the cake is cool, trickle the icing (frosting) over the top and decorate with glacé (candied) cherry and walnut halves. Serve plain or spread with butter.

Makes one 1 kg/2 lb loaf

Apricot Almond Loaf

METRIC/IMPERIAL

350 g/12 oz self-raising flour
½ teaspoon salt
75 g/3 oz caster sugar
150 g/5 oz dried apricots, soaked overnight and chopped
50 g/2 oz blanched almonds, coarsely chopped
grated rind of 1 lemon
2 eggs, beaten
8 to 9 tablespoons milk
50 g/2 oz butter, melted

Topping:

100 g/4 oz icing sugar, sifted
juice of 1 lemon
5 glacé apricots **or** 5 whole dried apricots, soaked, then stewed in syrup and well drained angelica strips, cut into leaves

AMERICAN

3 cups self-rising flour
½ teaspoon salt
⅓ cup sugar
1 cup dried apricots, soaked overnight and chopped
½ cup coarsely chopped blanched almonds
grated rind of 1 lemon
2 eggs, beaten
8 to 9 tablespoons milk
¼ cup butter, melted

Topping:

1 cup confectioners' sugar, sifted
juice of 1 lemon
5 candied apricots, **or** 5 whole dried apricots, soaked, then stewed in syrup and well drained angelica strips cut into leaves

Grease and line the bottom of a 1 kg/2 lb loaf tin (loaf pan). Sift the flour and salt into a bowl, add the sugar, apricots, almonds and the lemon rind. Make a well in the centre. Blend together the eggs, milk and melted butter, then stir into the flour to make a soft dropping consistency. Turn into the prepared tin and bake in a preheated moderate oven (160°C/325°F, Gas Mark 3) for 1½ hours. Turn out and cool on a wire rack.

To make the topping, put the icing sugar (confectioners' sugar) in a bowl and beat in enough lemon juice to make a thin coating consistency. Spread half over the top of the loaf. Place the apricots down the centre and arrange the angelica leaves along either side. If necessary, thin down the remainder of the icing (frosting) with a little more lemon juice, then trickle over the apricots to give a criss-cross effect and allow a little to run down the sides of the loaf.

Makes one 1 kg/2 lb loaf

Fruit Teabread

METRIC/IMPERIAL	AMERICAN
100 g/4 oz butter	$\frac{1}{2}$ cup butter
75 g/3 oz brown sugar	$\frac{1}{2}$ cup brown sugar
100 g/4 oz black treacle	$\frac{1}{3}$ cup molasses
3 eggs	3 eggs
225 g/8 oz flour	2 cups all-purpose flour
1 teaspoon bicarbonate soda	1 teaspoon baking soda
2 teaspoons ground ginger	2 teaspoons ground ginger
$\frac{1}{2}$ teaspoon grated nutmeg	$\frac{1}{2}$ teaspoon grated nutmeg
50 g/2 oz rolled oats	$\frac{2}{3}$ cup rolled oats
75 g/3 oz sultanas	$\frac{1}{2}$ cup seedless white raisins
25 g/1 oz flaked almonds	$\frac{1}{4}$ cup slivered almonds
175 ml/6 fl oz soured cream	$\frac{3}{4}$ cup sour cream

Place the butter, sugar and black treacle (molasses) in a saucepan and heat over a moderate flame until the butter has melted. Set aside to cool slightly, then beat in the eggs, one at a time. Sift the flour, bicarbonate of soda (baking soda) and spices into a bowl, then stir in the oats, sultanas (seedless white raisins) and almonds. Add the butter mixture and the cream and stir well.

Line an 18 cm/7 in square baking tin (pan) with a double thickness of greased greaseproof paper (or non-stick parchment paper). Spoon in the batter. Bake in a preheated moderate oven (180°C/350°F, Gas Mark 4) for 50 minutes to 1 hour, or until a knife inserted into the centre comes out clean. Cool on a wire rack.

Makes one 18 cm/7 in square cake

HONEY CINNAMON BUNS (page 71) (Photograph: Gale's Honey)

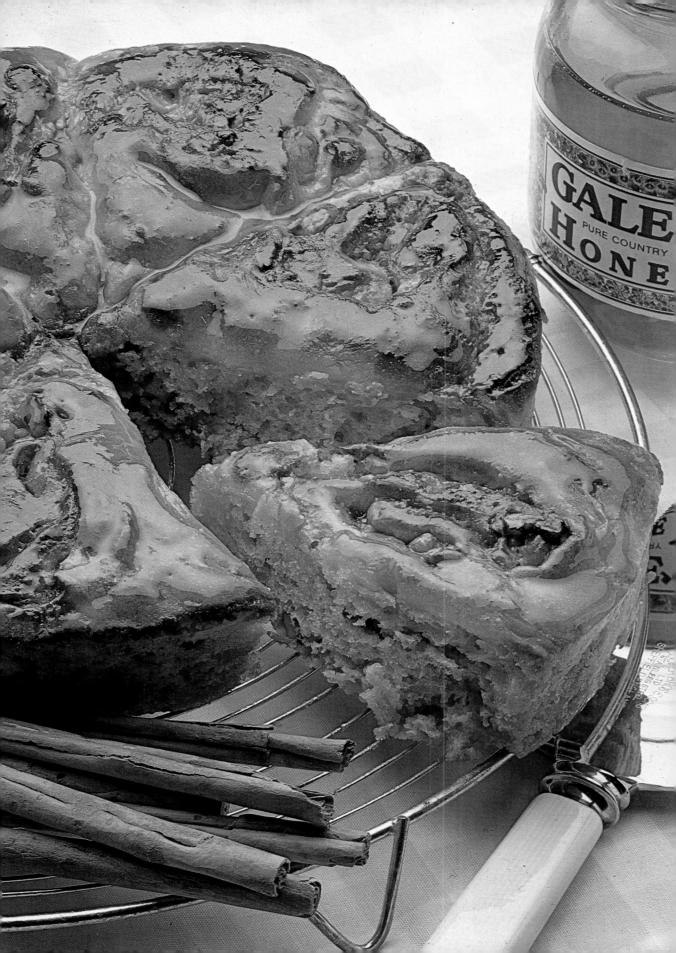

Drop Scones

METRIC/IMPERIAL	AMERICAN
a little lard	a little shortening
225 g/8 oz self-raising flour	2 cups self-rising flour
2 teaspoons baking powder	2 teaspoons baking powder
25 g/1 oz caster sugar	2 tablespoons firmly packed sugar
pinch of salt	pinch of salt
1 tablespoon golden syrup	1 tablespoon maple syrup
1 egg, beaten	1 egg, beaten
200 ml/$\frac{1}{3}$ pint plus	$\frac{7}{8}$ cup plus 1 tablespoon milk
1 tablespoon milk	

Prepare a griddle or very strong frying pan (skillet) by lightly greasing it with lard (shortening) and place it over a medium heat to become moderately hot.

Sift together the flour and baking powder into a bowl, add the remaining ingredients and mix together with a wooden spoon to a fairly thick batter.

Drop tablespoons of the batter on to the hot griddle, or frying pan (skillet) about 5 cm/2 in apart. Cook over a moderate heat until golden and bubbles appear on the surface. Turn with a palette knife and cook the other side. Continue the process with the remaining batter. Place the cooked scones on one half of a clean cloth and fold the other half over to keep them hot and moist.

Serve hot or cold, spread with butter or margarine.

Makes about 25 to 30 scones

Scottish Treacle Scones

METRIC/IMPERIAL	AMERICAN
500 g/1 lb plain flour	4 cups all-purpose flour
1 teaspoon bicarbonate of soda	1 teaspoon baking soda
$\frac{1}{2}$ teaspoon cream of tartar	$\frac{1}{2}$ teaspoon cream of tartar
1 teaspoon ground cinnamon	1 teaspoon ground cinnamon
1 teaspoon mixed spice	1 teaspoon mixed spice
$\frac{1}{2}$ teaspoon salt	$\frac{1}{2}$ teaspoon salt
50 g/2 oz butter or margarine	$\frac{1}{4}$ cup butter or margarine
2 teaspoons sugar	2 teaspoons sugar
2 tablespoons black treacle	2 tablespoons molasses
300 ml/$\frac{1}{2}$ pint milk	$1\frac{1}{4}$ cups milk
To glaze:	**To glaze:**
milk	milk

Sift together all the dry ingredients, except the sugar, in a bowl. Rub in the butter until the mixture resembles fine breadcrumbs, then add the sugar and treacle (molasses). Mix to a soft dough with the milk. Turn out on to a lightly floured board, knead lightly then roll out to 1 cm/½ in thickness. Cut into 8 cm/3 in triangles and brush the tops with milk.

Bake in a preheated hot oven (220°C/425°F, Gas Mark 7) for about 15 minutes. Serve fresh from the oven, while still warm, with butter.

Makes 10 scones

Apple and Walnut Bread

METRIC/IMPERIAL
50 g/2 oz butter or margarine
100 g/4 oz caster sugar
1 egg, beaten
150 ml/¼ pint apple purée, unsweetened
175 g/6 oz plain flour
½ teaspoon salt
1 teaspoon bicarbonate of soda
175 g/6 oz wholemeal flour
120 ml/4 fl oz milk
3 tablespoons soured cream
50 g/2 oz chopped walnuts

AMERICAN
¼ cup butter or margarine
½ cup sugar
1 egg, beaten
⅔ cup apple sauce, unsweetened
1½ cups all-purpose flour
½ teaspoon salt
1 teaspoon baking soda
1½ cups wholewheat flour
½ cup milk
3 tablespoons sour cream
½ cup chopped walnuts

Cream the butter and sugar together until well blended. Beat in the egg and the apple purée (apple sauce). Sift together the plain (all-purpose) flour, salt and bicarbonate of soda (baking soda) and add the wholemeal (wholewheat) flour. Mix together the milk and cream and add to the apple mixture alternately with the flour. Fold in the chopped nuts.

Place the dough in two 500 g/1 lb loaf tins (loaf pans) or one 1 kg/2 lb loaf tin (loaf pan). Bake in a preheated moderate oven (180°C/350°F, Gas Mark 4) for about 1¼ hours. Leave to cool in the tin (pan).

Makes one 1 kg/2 lb loaf or two 500 g/1 lb loaves

Cream Scones

METRIC/IMPERIAL
150 g/5 oz plain flour
½ teaspoon salt
2 teaspoons baking powder
150 ml/5 fl oz single cream
3 tablespoons raspberry jam
150 ml/5 fl oz double cream

AMERICAN
1¼ cups all-purpose flour
½ teaspoon salt
2 teaspoons baking powder
⅔ cup light cream
3 tablespoons raspberry preserve
⅔ cup heavy cream

Sift together the dry ingredients and stir in the single (light) cream to make an elastic dough. Knead lightly and roll out on to a floured board to 1 cm/½ in thickness and cut into rounds with a 5 cm/2 in cutter.

Place on a greased and floured baking sheet and bake in a preheated hot oven (220°C/425°F, Gas Mark 7) for 12 to 15 minutes until well risen and golden brown. Cool on a wire rack.

Just before serving, split and fill with jam and whipped cream.
Makes 9 scones

Norfolk Scone

METRIC/IMPERIAL
500 g/1 lb self-raising flour
1 teaspoon salt
100 g/4 oz butter or margarine
2 eggs, beaten
200 ml/⅓ pint plus 1 tablespoon milk
Filling:
25 g/1 oz butter or margarine,
  softened
100 g/4 oz currants
½ teaspoon grated nutmeg
100 g/4 oz demerara sugar

AMERICAN
4 cups self-rising flour
1 teaspoon salt
½ cup butter or margarine
2 eggs, beaten
⅞ cup plus 1 tablespoon milk
Filling:
2 tablespoons softened butter or
  margarine
⅔ cup currants
½ teaspoon grated nutmeg
⅔ cup light brown sugar

Sift together the flour and salt. Rub in the butter until the mixture resembles fine breadcrumbs. Mix to a soft dough with the eggs and milk. Turn on to a floured board and knead lightly. Divide in half and roll each section out into a 20 cm/8 in circle about 2 cm/¾ in thick. Lift one circle on to a baking sheet and spread the top with butter. Mix the currants, nutmeg and 75 g/3 oz/½ cup of the demerara (light brown) sugar together and sprinkle this mixture over the butter. Place the second circle on top, mark and cut almost through into eight wedges. Brush with milk and sprinkle over the remaining sugar.

Bake in a preheated moderately hot oven (200°C/400°F, Gas Mark 6) for about 50 minutes
Makes one 20 cm/8 in round scone

68

HOT APPLE MUFFINS *(page 70) (Photograph: Apple and Pear Development Council)*

Hot Apple Muffins

METRIC/IMPERIAL
Topping:
4 medium red dessert apples
3 tablespoons caster sugar
2 teaspoons ground cinnamon
Muffin mixture:
225 g/8 oz plain flour
1 teaspoon salt
1 tablespoon baking powder
50 g/2 oz caster sugar
2 eggs
150 ml/¼ pint milk
50 g/2 oz melted butter
75 g/3 oz peeled and chopped dessert
  apples

AMERICAN
Topping:
4 medium red dessert apples
3 tablespoons sugar
2 teaspoons ground cinnamon
Muffin batter:
2 cups all-purpose flour
1 teaspoon salt
1 tablespoon baking powder
¼ cup sugar
2 eggs
⅔ cup milk
¼ cup melted butter
1 cup peeled and chopped dessert
apples

To prepare the topping, core and peel the apples, keeping them whole.
Cut each one into four or five thick rings. Mix the sugar and cinnamon
together and coat the apple rings. Reserve.

To make the muffin mixture, sift together the dry ingredients in a
mixing bowl. In another bowl beat the eggs, add the milk and melted
butter. Stir the liquid very quickly into the flour mixture – do not beat
and do not worry about lumps. Speed is essential. Fold in the chopped
apples. Fill 24 × 5 cm/2 in greased bun tins (bun shells) or paper cases,
filled to one-third, and put one cinnamon apple ring on each muffin.

Bake in a preheated hot oven (220°C/425°F, Gas Mark 7) for 15 to 25
minutes, until cooked. Remove from tins (shells) and serve hot.
Makes 20 to 24 muffins

Honey Cinnamon Buns

METRIC/IMPERIAL
2 tablespoons hand-hot water
4 tablespoons hand-hot milk
50 g/2 oz sugar
2 teaspoons dried yeast
75 g/3 oz butter, melted
1 teaspoon salt
1 egg, beaten
225 g/8 oz plain flour
3 tablespoons clear honey
4 teaspoons cinnamon
50 g/2 oz chopped walnuts

AMERICAN
2 tablespoons hand-hot water
¼ cup hand-hot milk
¼ cup sugar
2 teaspoons active dry yeast
⅜ cup melted butter
1 teaspoon salt
1 egg, beaten
2 cups all-purpose flour
3 tablespoons clear honey
4 teaspoons cinnamon
½ cup chopped walnuts

Put the water and milk in a bowl, stir in the sugar and sprinkle in the dried yeast. Put in a warm place until frothy.

Mix the butter, salt and egg together. Put the flour in a large bowl and make a well in the centre. Pour in the yeast and butter mixtures and mix in the flour until the dough is well combined. Take the dough out of the bowl and knead on a floured surface for 5 minutes until the dough is smooth and elastic.

Grease a mixing bowl or the inside of a large polythene (plastic) bag, then put in the ball of dough. Cover and leave in a warm place for 1 hour or until double in size.

Turn out of the bowl, knead and roll the dough into an oblong about 20 × 30 cm/8 × 12 in. Spread over the honey and sprinkle with cinnamon and walnuts and roll up from the long end. Slice the roll quite thickly into 7 pieces and lay slices flat to form a circle in a greased 20 cm/8 in round sandwich tin (layer cake pan). Brush the top with a little butter and set aside in a warm place for about 30 minutes, or until the buns have risen and almost doubled in bulk.

Bake in a preheated moderately hot oven (190°C/375°F, Gas Mark 5) for about 25 minutes or until golden brown. When cooked the individual slices can be broken off (or cut) to serve.

Makes 7 buns

Shrove Tuesday Buns

METRIC/IMPERIAL

500 g/1 lb plain flour
½ teaspoon salt
200 g/7 oz butter
65 g/2½ oz caster sugar
75 g/3 oz raisins
50 g/2 oz mixed peel
1 teaspoon mixed spice
Yeast liquid:
175 ml/6 fl oz milk
50 g/2 oz fresh yeast, (do not use
  dried yeast for this method)
25 mg ascorbic acid tablet
2 eggs, beaten
To decorate:
a little melted butter
crushed sugar cubes

AMERICAN

4 cups all-purpose flour
½ teaspoon salt
¾ cup plus 2 tablespoons butter
5 tablespoons firmly packed sugar
½ cup raisins
⅓ cup candied peel
1 teaspoon mixed spice
Yeast liquid:
¾ cup milk
2 cakes compressed yeast (do not use
  active dry yeast for this method)
25 mg ascorbic acid tablet
2 eggs, beaten
To decorate:
a little melted butter
crushed sugar cubes

Place the flour and salt in a large bowl. Rub in the butter until the mixture resembles fine breadcrumbs. Add the sugar, raisins, mixed peel (candied peel) and mixed spice; stir in.

Warm the milk slightly and add the yeast and ascorbic acid tablet, stir until dissolved. Add the eggs to the yeast liquid, pour into the dry ingredients and mix well, using a wooden spoon, until mixture forms a soft dough.

Turn the dough out on to a lightly floured surface and knead well for about 10 minutes until the dough is smooth and no longer sticky. Place in a lightly greased polythene (plastic) bag and leave for five minutes.

Cut dough into 40 g/1½ oz pieces, shape into rounds and place on greased baking sheets, allowing plenty of space between rounds. Cover the buns with greased polythene (plastic) bags and leave in a warm place until buns have doubled in size, about 40 minutes. Remove bags and bake the buns in a preheated moderately hot oven (190°C/375°F, Gas Mark 5) for 15 minutes until golden brown. Remove and cool on a wire rack. Spread the tops of the buns very lightly with the butter, and roll them in crushed sugar cubes.

Makes about 20 buns

From top, clockwise: SHROVE TUESDAY BUNS, SANDCAKE *(page 19),* VANILLA BUTTER BISCUITS *(page 60) (Photograph: The Danish Centre, London)*

Hot Cross Buns

METRIC/IMPERIAL

500 g/1 lb plain flour
$\frac{1}{4}$ teaspoon salt
2 teaspoons mixed spice
100 g/4 oz margarine
100 g/4 oz caster sugar
175 g/6 oz currants
50 g/2 oz chopped mixed peel
15 g/$\frac{1}{2}$ oz dried yeast
300 ml/$\frac{1}{2}$ pint warm milk

To decorate:
1 tablespoon plain flour
cold water

To glaze:
2 tablespoons milk
2 tablespoons sugar

AMERICAN

4 cups all-purpose flour
$\frac{1}{4}$ teaspoon salt
2 teaspoons mixed spice
$\frac{1}{2}$ cup margarine
$\frac{1}{2}$ cup sugar
1 cup currants
$\frac{1}{3}$ cup chopped candied peel
4 teaspoons active dry yeast
$1\frac{1}{4}$ cups warm milk

To decorate:
1 tablespoon all-purpose flour
cold water

To glaze:
2 tablespoons milk
2 tablespoons sugar

Sift the flour, salt and mixed spice into a bowl. Rub the margarine into the flour until the mixture resembles fine breadcrumbs. Add the sugar, currants and mixed peel and mix thoroughly. Sprinkle the yeast on to the warm milk and whisk until dissolved. Make a well in the centre of the flour mixture and pour in the milk and yeast. Sprinkle a little extra flour over the milk and stand the bowl in a warm place until bubbles appear on the surface, 30 to 45 minutes. Beat the mixture thoroughly until it leaves the side of the bowl and is smooth.

Cover and allow to rise until double in bulk, 30 to 45 minutes. Turn on to a floured board and knead lightly. Divide into 16 pieces and shape into rounds. Place on a greased baking sheet, cover with greased polythene (plastic) and allow to rise for 20 to 30 minutes.

To decorate, mix the flour with just enough water to form a soft paste. Place in a piping bag (pastry bag) with a fine nozzle and pipe crosses on the buns (or cut crosses with a sharp knife). Bake in a preheated hot oven (220°C/425°F, Gas Mark 7) for 15 to 20 minutes until well browned.

Glaze immediately. Make the glaze by dissolving together the milk and sugar over a low heat. Brush over the buns on removal from the oven.

Makes about 16 buns

Devonshire Splits

METRIC/IMPERIAL

Yeast liquid:
1 teaspoon sugar
300 ml/½ pint warm milk
4 teaspoons dried yeast

Dough:
50 g/2 oz margarine
500 g/1 lb plain flour, sifted
40 g/1½ oz caster sugar
1 teaspoon salt

Filling:
strawberry jam
150 ml/5 fl oz double cream, whipped

To decorate:
sifted icing sugar

AMERICAN

Yeast liquid:
1 teaspoon sugar
1¼ cups warm milk
4 teaspoons active dry yeast

Dough:
¼ cup margarine
4 cups all-purpose flour, sifted
3 tablespoons firmly packed sugar
1 teaspoon salt

Filling:
strawberry preserve
⅔ cup heavy cream, whipped

To decorate:
sifted confectioners' sugar

To make the yeast liquid, dissolve the sugar in the warm milk, sprinkle on the yeast, whisk well and leave until frothy, about 10 minutes. Melt the margarine and cool. Place the flour, sugar and salt in a bowl. Add the margarine and the yeast liquid and mix together with a palette knife to a fairly stiff dough. Turn on to a floured surface and knead until smooth. Leave the dough, covered, in a warm place to rise until doubled in size, 40 to 45 minutes.

Knead the dough again and divide into 12 pieces. Shape each into a round bun and place on a greased baking sheet. Cover with greased polythene (plastic) and leave in a warm place to rise, 20 minutes. Remove the polythene (plastic).

Bake the buns in the centre of a preheated hot oven (230°C/450°F, Gas Mark 8) for 10 to 12 minutes. Place on a wire rack to cool.

To fill; make a diagonal cut through the centre of each bun. Open them out and spread one half of each with jam and the other half with cream. Sandwich together. Dust each bun with icing sugar (confectioners' sugar).

Makes 12 round buns

Cream Buns

METRIC/IMPERIAL
Choux pastry:
50 g/2 oz butter
150 ml/¼ pint water
65 g/2½ oz plain flour
small pinch salt
2 eggs
Filling:
300 ml/½ pint double cream, whipped
To decorate:
sifted icing sugar

AMERICAN
Choux pastry:
¼ cup butter
⅔ cup water
½ cup plus 2 tablespoons all-purpose flour
small pinch of salt
2 eggs
Filling:
1¼ cups heavy cream, whipped
To decorate:
sifted confectioners' sugar

Melt the butter in the water in a saucepan and bring to the boil. Remove from the heat immediately and beat in the flour and salt with a wooden spoon until the dough is smooth. Return to a low heat and continue to beat until the dough forms a ball and leaves the sides of the pan clean. Cool the dough slightly and beat in the eggs one at a time until completely absorbed and the mixture is very smooth and shiny.

Using a large fluted nozzle, pipe the dough on to a greased baking sheet in bun shapes about 4 cm/1½ in apart to leave room for rising. (Or use a spoon to make bun shapes.)

Bake above the middle of a preheated moderately hot oven (200°C/400°F, Gas Mark 6) for 20 minutes, or until risen and golden. Turn the heat down to 190°C/375°F, Gas Mark 5 for 10 to 15 minutes. Remove from the oven, split open to allow the steam to escape and return to the oven for 5 minutes to dry out. Cool on a wire rack. When cold, fill with whipped cream and dust with icing sugar (confectioners' sugar).
Makes about 10 cream buns

CREAM BUNS *(Photograph: British Egg Information Service)*

BREADS AND YEAST RECIPES

Panettone

METRIC/IMPERIAL
Yeast liquid:
1 teaspoon caster sugar
150 ml/¼ pint warm water
1 tablespoon dried yeast
Dough:
400 g/14 oz strong plain white flour
½ teaspoon salt
25 g/1 oz caster sugar
100 g/4 oz butter or margarine
3 egg yolks
½ teaspoon vanilla essence
grated rind of ¼ lemon
50 g/2 oz raisins
50 g/2 oz sultanas
50 g/2 oz mixed peel
To glaze:
25 g/1 oz butter, melted

AMERICAN
Yeast liquid:
1 teaspoon sugar
⅔ cup warm water
1 tablespoon active dry yeast
Dough:
3½ cups all-purpose flour
½ teaspoon salt
2 tablespoons firmly packed sugar
½ cup butter or margarine
3 egg yolks
½ teaspoon vanilla extract
grated rind of ¼ lemon
6 tablespoons raisins
6 tablespoons seedless white raisins
6 tablespoons candied peel
To glaze:
2 tablespoons butter, melted

To make the yeast liquid, dissolve the sugar in the water. Sprinkle the yeast on top and leave in a warm place for 10 minutes until frothy.

To make the dough, combine the flour, salt and sugar in a large bowl. Rub in the fat until the mixture resembles fine breadcrumbs. Gradually beat in the yeast liquid with the egg yolks, vanilla essence (vanilla extract) and grated lemon rind to form a firm dough. (Do not add the fruit). Turn the dough on to a lightly floured working surface and knead thoroughly for about 10 minutes. Shape into a ball. Place the dough in a large bowl covered with lightly oiled polythene (plastic) and leave to rise until double in size, about 1½ hours at room temperature.

Turn the dough on to a lightly floured working surface and gradually knead in the fruit. Continue kneading until smooth and firm, about 5 minutes. Shape to fit a lightly greased 18 cm/7 in deep round cake tin (cake pan). Cover with lightly oiled polythene (plastic) and leave to rise in a warm place until the dough reaches the top of the tin (pan).

Uncover and bake in a preheated moderately hot oven (200°C/400°F, Gas Mark 6) for 20 minutes. Reduce the temperature to moderate (180°C/350°F, Gas Mark 4) and bake for a further 40 minutes. Cool on a wire rack, brushing with melted butter while still warm.
Makes about 8 to 10 slices

Peach and Brown Sugar Roll

METRIC/IMPERIAL

Yeast liquid:
1 teaspoon sugar
150 ml/¼ pint warm water
2 teaspoons dried yeast

Dough:
225 g/8 oz strong plain white flour
pinch of salt
15 g/½ oz butter or margarine

Filling:
2 tablespoons peach jam, warmed and sieved
25 g/1 oz soft brown sugar
½ teaspoon ground cinnamon
1 × 425 g/15 oz can peaches, well drained and chopped

Topping:
a little milk
1 tablespoon soft brown sugar

AMERICAN

Yeast liquid:
1 teaspoon sugar
⅔ cup warm water
2 teaspoons active dry yeast

Dough:
2 cups all-purpose flour
pinch of salt
1 tablespoon butter

Filling:
2 tablespoons peach preserve, warmed and strained
2 tablespoons firmly packed light brown sugar
½ teaspoon ground cinnamon
1 × 1 lb can peaches, well drained and chopped

Topping:
a little milk
1 tablespoon light brown sugar

To make the yeast liquid, dissolve the sugar in the water, sprinkle the yeast on top and leave in a warm place for about 10 minutes until frothy.

To make the dough, combine the flour and salt in a bowl. Rub in the fat until the mixture resembles fine breadcrumbs. Add the yeast liquid, mixing to a firm dough. Turn the dough on to a lightly floured working surface and knead for about 10 minutes until dough is firm and elastic. Place in a large bowl covered with lightly oiled polythene (plastic) and leave to rise until double in size, about 1½ to 2 hours at average room temperature.

Uncover and knead for a further two minutes. Roll out to a rectangle 16 × 30 cm/8 × 12 in. Brush with the jam and sprinkle with sugar, cinnamon and peaches. Roll up like a Swiss roll (jelly roll) and place in a lightly greased 500 g/1 lb loaf tin (loaf pan). Cover with lightly oiled polythene (plastic) and leave to rise until the dough reaches the top of the loaf tin (loaf pan).

Uncover, brush with milk and sprinkle with soft brown sugar (light brown sugar). Bake in a preheated moderately hot oven (200°C/400°F, Gas Mark 6) for about 30 minutes until firm to the touch and golden brown. Cool on a wire rack and serve in buttered slices.

Makes about 8 to 10 slices

Spider's Web Ring

METRIC/IMPERIAL

Yeast liquid:

1 teaspoon sugar
150 ml/¼ pint warm water
2 teaspoons dried yeast

Dough:

225 g/8 oz strong plain white flour
pinch of salt
15 g/½ oz butter
50 g/2 oz sultanas
25 g/1 oz mixed peel

Glaze and topping:

50 g/2 oz sugar
150 ml/¼ pint water
25 g/1 oz mixed nuts, chopped
50 g/2 oz glacé cherries, chopped
100 g/4 oz icing sugar, sifted
1 tablespoon water

AMERICAN

Yeast liquid:

1 teaspoon sugar
⅔ cup warm water
2 teaspoons active dry yeast

Dough:

2 cups all-purpose flour
pinch of salt
1 tablespoon butter
6 tablespoons seedless white raisins
3 tablespoons candied peel

Glaze and topping:

¼ cup sugar
⅔ cup water
¼ cup mixed chopped nuts
¼ cup chopped candied cherries
1 cup sifted confectioners' sugar
1 tablespoon water

To make the yeast liquid, dissolve the sugar in the water, sprinkle the dried yeast on top and leave in a warm place until frothy, for about 10 minutes.

To make the dough, combine the flour and salt in a bowl. Rub in the butter until the mixture resembles fine breadcrumbs. Stir in the fruit, mixing well. Beat in the yeast liquid, mixing to a firm dough. Turn on to a lightly floured working surface and knead for 10 minutes until firm and no longer sticky. Place in a large bowl covered with lightly oiled polythene (plastic) and leave to rise until double in size, about 1½ to 2 hours at average room temperature.

Uncover and knead for a further two minutes. Roll out into a 25 cm/10 in circle and place on a lightly greased baking sheet. Cover with lightly oiled polythene (plastic) and leave to rise in a warm place for 45 to 60 minutes, until double in size. Uncover and bake in a preheated moderately hot oven (200°C/400°F, Gas Mark 6) for 20 to 25 minutes.

To glaze, dissolve the sugar in the water and brush over the bread while it is still warm. Sprinkle the nuts and glacé cherries (candied cherries) over the top and leave to cool on a wire rack. Mix the icing sugar (confectioners' sugar) and water together to a smooth consistency and trickle over the bread in the shape of a spider's web.

Serves 8 to 10

From top, clockwise: GOLDEN SAVARIN (page 15), SPIDER'S WEBB RING, PEACH AND BROWN SUGAR ROLL (page 79), PANETTONE (page 78) (Photograph: The Homepride Kitchen)

Basic White Bread

METRIC/IMPERIAL

Yeast liquid:

1 teaspoon sugar
300 ml/½ pint warm milk
2 teaspoons dried yeast

Dough:

500 g/1 lb plain flour
1 teaspoon salt
50 g/2 oz lard or margarine

AMERICAN

Yeast liquid:

1 teaspoon sugar
1¼ cups warm milk
2 teaspoons active dry yeast

Dough:

4 cups all-purpose flour
1 teaspoon salt
¼ cup shortening or margarine

To make the yeast liquid, dissolve the sugar in warm milk, sprinkle on the yeast, whisk well and leave until frothy, about 10 minutes.

Step 1. Mix the flour and salt together in a bowl and rub in the fat. Add the yeast liquid and work to a firm dough, until the sides of the bowl are left clean.

Step 2. Turn the dough on to a lightly floured working surface and knead thoroughly by folding the dough towards you and then pushing it down and away with the palm of the hand. Continue kneading, until the dough is firm, elastic and no longer sticky, about 10 minutes.

Step 3. Shape the dough into a ball, place in a mixing bowl and cover with oiled polythene (plastic). Leave to rise until the dough is double in size and springs back when pressed gently with a floured finger. Rising times vary with temperature: a quick rise – about 45 to 60 minutes in a warm place; a slow rise – about 2 hours at average room temperature; a cold rise – about 12 to 24 hours in a refrigerator (return the dough to room temperature before shaping). Have ready a greased loaf tin (loaf pan) 23 × 18 × 8 cm/9 × 7 × 3½ in.

Step 4. Turn the risen dough on to a lightly floured working surface, flatten with the knuckles to knock out the air bubbles and knead until firm, about 2 minutes. Press the dough into an oblong the same width as the loaf tin (loaf pan). Fold into three and turn over so the seam is underneath. Smooth over the top, tuck in the ends and place in the tin (pan).

Dust the top of dough with flour and place the tin (pan) in a large, lightly oiled polythene (plastic) bag and leave until the dough is double in size or rises to the top of the tin (pan). It will take 30 to 40 minutes in a warm place, 1 to 1¼ hours at room temperature, 12 to 24 hours in a refrigerator. Remove the polythene (plastic) bag.

Bake in a preheated hot oven (220°C/425°F, Gas Mark 7) for 45 to 50 minutes until well risen and a deep golden brown. Cooked loaves shrink slightly from the sides of the tin (pan) and sound hollow when tapped underneath with the knuckles. Remove from the tin (pan) and cool on a wire rack.

Makes about 750 g/1½ lb dough

Cheesy Whirls

METRIC/IMPERIAL
500 g/1 lb risen white bread dough
Filling:
25 g/1 oz butter, melted
100 g/4 oz Cheddar cheese, grated
To glaze:
1 egg, beaten
1 teaspoon sugar
1 tablespoon water

AMERICAN
1 lb risen white bread dough
Filling:
2 tablespoons butter, melted
¼ lb Cheddar cheese, grated
To glaze:
1 egg, beaten
1 teaspoon sugar
1 tablespoon water

Cut off and weigh 500 g/1 lb risen basic dough after the first rising. Knead the dough until smooth and roll out to an oblong 30 × 25 cm/12 × 9 in. Brush with the melted butter and sprinkle with the cheese. Roll up from the longest side and dampen the edge with water to seal. Cut into nine slices. Place in a greased 18 cm/7 in cake tin (pan).

To make the glaze, blend together the egg, sugar and water. Brush the top with glaze. Cover with lightly oiled polythene (plastic) and leave to rise for about 30 minutes in a warm place until the dough feels springy. Bake in a preheated moderately hot oven (190°C/375°F, Gas Mark 5) for 30 minutes until well risen and golden.

Makes 9 buns

Cherry Surprise Bun Ring

METRIC/IMPERIAL
500 g/1 lb risen white bread dough
8 squares of chocolate
To glaze:
1 egg, beaten
1 teaspoon sugar
1 tablespoon water
To decorate:
50 g/2 oz glacé cherries, chopped
50 g/2 oz flaked almonds, toasted

AMERICAN
1 lb risen white bread dough
8 squares of chocolate
To glaze:
1 egg, beaten
1 teaspoon sugar
1 tablespoon water
To decorate:
¼ cup chopped candied cherries
¼ cup slivered almonds, toasted

Cut off and weigh 500 g/1 lb of the basic dough after the first rising. Knead until smooth. Divide into eight pieces; shape each into a ball. Push a square of chocolate into the centre of each, seal the dough and reshape. Arrange the balls in a circle on a well greased baking sheet.

Glaze as for Cheesy Whirls, cover and leave to rise for 30 minutes. Bake in a moderately hot oven (190°C/375°F, Gas Mark 5) for about 30 minutes. Sprinkle the top with the cherries and almonds.

Makes 8 buns

Almond and Raisin Plait

METRIC/IMPERIAL
basic white bread ingredients (see
  page 82)
175 g/6 oz raisins
50 g/2 oz almonds, chopped
rind and juice of 1 orange
To glaze:
1 egg, beaten
1 tablespoon sugar
1 tablespoon water
To decorate:
rind of 1 orange
50 g/2 oz sugar
4 tablespoons water
25 g/1 oz flaked almonds

AMERICAN
basic white bread ingredients (see
  page 82)
1 cup raisins
½ cup chopped almonds
rind and juice of 1 orange
To glaze:
1 egg, beaten
1 tablespoon sugar
1 tablespoon water
To decorate:
rind of 1 orange
¼ cup sugar
4 tablespoons water
¼ cup slivered almonds

Make up the dough as instructed up to step 4, adding the raisins,
chopped almonds and juice of the orange to the flour mixture before
mixing in the yeast liquid (step 1). Reserve the orange rind. Turn risen
dough on to a floured surface and knead until smooth. Divide into two.
Divide one piece of dough into three. Roll each piece into a strand
about 30 cm/12 in long and join the strands together at one end. Place
on a baking sheet, plait loosely and tuck the ends underneath.

To make the glaze, blend together the egg, sugar and water. Brush
the top with the glaze. Repeat with the other piece of dough. Cover
both plaits with oiled polythene (plastic) and leave to rise until double
in size, about 30 minutes, in a warm place.

Remove the polythene (plastic) and bake in a preheated moderately
hot oven (190°C/375°F, Gas Mark 5) for 30 to 35 minutes. To make the
topping, cut the orange rind, without the pith, into thin strips. Dissolve
the sugar in the water, add the orange rind, bring to the boil, reduce
the heat and cook until the orange rind is tender and the syrup is
reduced by half. Spoon the orange rind and syrup over the warm loaves
and sprinkle the flaked (slivered) almonds on top.
Makes 2 plaits

From top, clockwise: CHERRY SURPRISE BUN RING (page 83),
ALMOND AND RAISIN PLAIT, CHEESY WHIRLS (page 83)
(Photograph: The Flour Advisory Bureau)

Basic Wholemeal (Wholewheat) Bread

METRIC/IMPERIAL

Yeast liquid:

1 teaspoon sugar
450 ml/¾ pint warm water
1 tablespoon dried yeast

Dough:

750 g/1½ lb wholemeal flour
2 teaspoons salt
15 g/½ oz lard

To glaze:

a little beaten egg and water or milk

Topping:

crushed cornflakes, cracked wheat,
  oatmeal, chopped nuts, poppy seeds,
  sesame seeds or caraway seeds,
  according to choice

AMERICAN

Yeast liquid:

1 teaspoon sugar
2 cups warm water
1 tablespoon active dry yeast

Dough:

6 cups wholewheat flour
2 teaspoons salt
1 tablespoon shortening

To glaze:

a little beaten egg and water or milk

Topping:

crushed cornflakes, cracked wheat,
  oatmeal, chopped nuts, poppy seeds,
  sesame seeds or caraway seeds,
  according to choice

To make the yeast liquid, dissolve the sugar in the water and sprinkle the yeast on top. Leave in a warm place for 10 minutes until frothy.

To make the dough, combine the flour and salt in a bowl. Rub in the lard (shortening). Using a wooden spoon, beat the yeast liquid into the flour mixture to form a firm dough. Turn the dough on to a lightly floured working surface and knead until it is no longer sticky. Shape into a ball.

Place the dough in a bowl covered with lightly oiled polythene (plastic). Leave to rise until double in size and springy to the touch, approximately 1½ to 2 hours at average room temperature. Knock back (punch down) the dough and knead. For two 500 g/1 lb loaves, divide in half and shape to fit two lightly greased 500 g/1 lb loaf tins (loaf pans) or use a 1 kg/2 lb loaf tin (loaf pan).

Cover the shaped dough with an oiled polythene (plastic) bag and tie loosely. Leave to rise for about 45 minutes until doubled in size. Uncover, glaze with the beaten egg and water, or milk, and spread with the topping of your choice.

Bake in a preheated hot oven (230°C/450°F, Gas Mark 8) for 30 to 40 minutes until well risen and the loaf/loaves sounds hollow when tapped on the bottom. Cool on a wire rack.

Makes two 500 g/1 lb loaves or 1 kg/2 lb loaf

Cottage Loaf

METRIC/IMPERIAL
½ *basic quantity wholemeal bread*
  dough
To glaze:
a little beaten egg and water or milk

AMERICAN
½ *basic quantity wholewheat bread*
  dough
To glaze:
a little beaten egg and water or milk

Divide the bread dough into two pieces in the proportion of one-third to two-thirds. Knock back (punch down) the dough and knead each piece until firm. Using the palm of the hand, shape the larger piece into a round and place on a lightly greased baking sheet. Similarly, shape the smaller piece and place it on top of the larger round. Using the floured handle of a wooden spoon, pierce through the centre of the two rounds, joining them together.

Cover the shaped dough with a greased polythene (plastic) bag and tie loosely. Leave to rise for about 45 minutes, until double in size. Uncover, glaze with the beaten egg and water, or milk, and sprinkle with the topping of your choice.

Bake in a preheated hot oven (230°C/450°F, Gas Mark 8) for 30 to 40 minutes until well risen and the loaf sounds hollow when tapped on the bottom. Cool on a wire rack.
Makes one 500 g/1 lb round cottage loaf

Caterpillar Loaf

METRIC/IMPERIAL
½ *basic quantity wholemeal bread*
  dough
To glaze:
a little beaten egg and water, or milk

AMERICAN
½ *basic quantity wholewheat bread*
  dough
To glaze:
a little beaten egg and water, or milk

Divide the dough into four equal sized pieces. Knock back (punch down) the dough and knead each piece until firm. Using the palm of the hand, roll each piece into a ball by pressing down hard and then easing up as the dough forms a smooth ball. Place the pieces side by side in a lightly greased 500 g/1 lb loaf tin (loaf pan). Cover with oiled polythene (plastic) and leave to rise for about 1 to 1½ hours at average room temperature until the dough reaches the top of the tin (pan) or doubles in size. Uncover, glaze with beaten egg and water, or milk, and sprinkle with the topping of your choice.

Bake in a preheated hot oven (230°C/450°F, Gas Mark 8) for 30 to 40 minutes until well risen and the loaf sounds hollow when tapped on the bottom. Cool on a wire rack.
Makes one 500 g/1 lb loaf

Farmhouse Teacakes

METRIC/IMPERIAL	AMERICAN
Batter:	**Batter:**
1 tablespoon dried yeast	1 tablespoon active dry yeast
1 teaspoon sugar	1 teaspoon sugar
150 ml/¼ pint warm milk	⅔ cup warm milk
150 ml/7 tablespoons warm water	7 tablespoons warm water
100 g/4 oz wholemeal flour	1 cup wholewheat flour
Dough:	**Dough:**
350 g/12 oz wholemeal flour	3 cups wholewheat flour
1 teaspoon salt	1 teaspoon salt
½ teaspoon ground nutmeg	½ teaspoon ground nutmeg
½ teaspoon ground cinnamon	½ teaspoon ground cinnamon
1 teaspoon caraway seeds	1 teaspoon caraway seeds
50 g/2 oz butter	¼ cup butter
50 g/2 oz caster sugar	¼ cup sugar
50 g/2 oz mixed peel	6 tablespoons candied peel
100 g/4 oz raisins	⅔ cup raisins
1 egg, beaten	1 egg beaten
To glaze:	**To glaze:**
50 g/2 oz sugar	¼ cup sugar
4 tablespoons water	4 tablespoons water

To make the batter, stir the yeast and sugar into the milk and water, leave to stand for 5 minutes. Mix in the flour and leave in a warm place for about 20 minutes until frothy.

For the dough, mix together the flour, salt, spices and caraway seeds. Rub in the butter and stir in the sugar and fruit. Stir the flour mixture and egg into the batter and mix to a soft dough. Turn the dough out on to a floured working surface and knead until no longer sticky. Make into a ball. Cover the dough with oiled polythene (plastic) and leave to rise for about 1½ hours until doubled in size.

Uncover and turn the dough on to a lightly floured surface. Knead for two minutes. Divide the dough into 10 equal sized pieces. Shape into buns by using the palm of the hand and rolling each piece into a ball by pressing down hard and then easing up as the dough forms a smooth ball. Place well apart on greased baking sheets. Cover with lightly oiled polythene (plastic) and leave to rise until double in size.

Uncover and bake in a preheated hot oven (220°C/425°F, Gas Mark 7) for 15 to 20 minutes until well risen and golden brown. Make the glaze by dissolving together the sugar and water in a saucepan over a moderate heat. Brush the warm buns with the glaze.

Makes 10 teacakes

From top, clockwise: WHOLEWHEAT CATERPILLAR AND COTTAGE LOAVES *(page 87),* FARMHOUSE TEACAKES, ICED FRUIT PLAIT *(page 90) (Photograph: The Homepride Kitchen)*

Iced Fruit Plait

METRIC/IMPERIAL

Yeast liquid:
1 teaspoon caster sugar
150 ml/¼ pint warm milk
2 teaspoons dried yeast
Dough:
275 g/10 oz strong plain white flour
½ teaspoon caster sugar
pinch of salt
½ teaspoon mixed spice
25 g/1 oz currants
50 g/2 oz sultanas
25 g/1 oz butter or margarine
1 egg, beaten
Icing:
225 g/8 oz icing sugar
3 tablespoons water
Topping:
25 g/1 oz glacé cherries, chopped
1 tablespoon chopped almonds

AMERICAN

Yeast liquid:
1 teaspoon sugar
⅔ cup warm milk
2 teaspoons active dry yeast
Dough:
2½ cups all-purpose flour
½ teaspoon sugar
pinch of salt
½ teaspoon mixed spice
3 tablespoons currants
⅓ cup seedless white raisins
2 tablespoons butter or margarine
1 egg, beaten
Frosting:
2 cups confectioners' sugar
3 tablespoons water
Topping:
3 tablespoons chopped candied
  cherries
1 tablespoon chopped almonds

To make the yeast liquid, dissolve the sugar in the milk, sprinkle the yeast on top and leave in a warm place for 10 minutes until frothy.

To make the dough, combine the flour, sugar, salt, mixed spice, currants and sultanas (seedless white raisins) in a large bowl. Rub in the fat. Using a wooden spoon, beat the yeast liquid and egg into the flour to form a firm dough. Turn the dough on to a lightly floured working surface and knead for 10 minutes until the dough is firm and no longer sticky. Shape into a ball. Place the dough in a bowl and cover with lightly oiled polythene (plastic). Leave to rise for about 1 hour in a warm place, until double in size and springy to the touch.

Uncover the dough and turn on to a lightly floured surface. Knead for 2 minutes. Divide the dough into three equal sized pieces. Using your hands, roll into strips of equal length. Gather the ends together and plait. At each end, press the strips together gently to seal. Place the plait on a greased baking sheet, cover with lightly oiled polythene (plastic). Leave to rise until double in size and springy to the touch. Uncover and bake in a preheated moderately hot oven (190°C/375°F, Gas Mark 5) for 35 to 40 minutes until well risen and golden brown. Remove from the oven and cool on a wire rack.

To make the icing (frosting), place the sugar and water in a bowl and mix together until the icing (frosting) is smooth and shiny. Spread evenly over the fruit plait and sprinkle the topping over. Leave to set. Serve sliced, with butter if desired.
Serves 10

INDEX

INDEX

The editor would like to thank the following for their assistance in compiling this book:-

The African Groundnut Council; The Apple & Pear Development Council; Birds Eye Kitchens; The British Egg Information Service; Brown & Polson; The Butter Information Council; Cadbury Typhoo Food Advisory Service; The Danish Centre, London; Eden Vale; The Flour Advisory Bureau; Frank Cooper; Gale's Honey; The Home Baking Bureau; The Homepride Kitchen; Kraft Foods Limited, Mazola Pure Corn Oil; The National Dairy Council; Potato Marketing Board; Stork Cookery Service; Tate & Lyle Test Kitchens.

PDO 80-155